The Grasshopper Trap

Also by Patrick F. McManus

Kid Camping From Aaaaiii! to Zip
A Fine and Pleasant Misery
They Shoot Canoes, Don't They?
Never Sniff a Gift Fish

The
Grasshopper
Trap

PATRICK F. McMANUS

Holt, Rinehart and Winston   New York

Copyright © 1985 by Patrick F. McManus
All rights reserved, including the right to reproduce
this book or portions thereof in any form.
Published by Holt, Rinehart and Winston,
383 Madison Avenue, New York, New York 10017.
Published simultaneously in Canada by Holt, Rinehart
and Winston of Canada, Limited.

Library of Congress Cataloging in Publication Data
McManus, Patrick F.
The grasshopper trap.
1. Outdoor life—Anecdotes, facetiae, satire, etc.
2. Hunting—Anecdotes, facetiae, satire, etc.
3. Fishing—Anecdotes, facetiae, satire, etc.
I. Title.
GV191.6.M325   1985   796.5   84-29768
ISBN 0-03-000738-0

First Edition

Design by Kate Nichols
Printed in the United States of America
10 9 8 7 6 5 4 3 2 1

All stories in this book appeared previously as follows: In *Outdoor Life*:
"The Skunk Ladder"; "How to Go *Splat!*" (originally titled "Into Each Life
a Little Fall Must Reign"); "The Human Fuel Pump"; " 'Twas a Dark and
Dreary Night"; "Trailer Trials"; "The Grasshopper Trap"; "Get Lost!";
"Metamorphosis and Other Outdoor Phenomena Wives Don't Under-
stand" (originally titled "Metamorphosis and Other Outdoor Phenomena"); "The Swamp"; "A Hunker Is Not a Squat"; "Why Wives on Christmas
Mourn" (originally titled "I Heard the Wives on Christmas Mourn"); "The
Hunting Lesson"; "*Nincompoopery* and Other Group Terms" (originally
titled "Off On a Lark"); "Character Flaws" (originally titled "Flaws"); "Mean
Tents"; "Crick Ritual"; "Hunting Camp Etiquette"; "Stone Soup" (origi-
nally titled "The Runaways"); "The Wager"; "Sweet Sweet Sixteen"; "Down
and Way Out in Brazil"; "Strange Encounters of the Bird Kind"; "The
Outing"; "I, the Hunted." In *Gutmann Knife Annual*: "First Knife" (origi-
nally titled "That First Knife"). In *Field & Stream Hunting Annual*: "The
Case of the Missed Deer." In *Hunting Guns*: "Gunrunning" (originally titled
"How to Buy a Gun . . . Without Your Wife Finding Out"). In *Field &
Stream*: "Bad Company"; "Letters from Camp"; "Never Cry Snake!" (orig-
inally titled "Don't Never Cry Wuff").

ISBN 0-03-000738-0

To Clare Conley

who bought and published the first humor piece I ever wrote and without whose encouragement and counsel I would never have become a writer of short humor. Still, he meant well.

Contents

The Grasshopper Trap

The Skunk Ladder

Driving out to the country the other day, my wife, Bun, and I passed the aromatic remains of at least ten road-killed skunks.

"Must be a good year for skunks," I observed.

"Looks like a bad one for them, if you ask me," Bun said.

"I mean there's obviously a large skunk population this year," I sniffed, instantly realizing that I shouldn't have sniffed, because at that moment we were passing another skunk carcass.

Just then a live skunk scurried out in front of the car. I swerved to the left and back to the right, and we managed to screech safely around it. Bun screeches quite often but it was the first time I had screeched in years.

"Goodness, that was close!" Bun said. "What would you have done if you'd hit that skunk with the car?"

"The only decent thing," I replied. "I'd have stopped

and buried it in the ditch. I might even have buried the skunk along with it."

"You talk as if you've had a lot of experience with skunks," she said.

"You bet," I said. "Mostly when I was a kid. You mean I've never told you about the skunk ladder? Boy, do you have a treat in store for you!"

"Sorry I mentioned it," she mumbled, possibly in an attempt to conceal her intense interest in the bizarre tale.

As I told Bun, my friend Crazy Eddie Muldoon and I were sitting on the Muldoon corral fence one summer afternoon, trying to think of something to do. This was shortly after I had nearly drowned in the creek while testing Eddie's deep-sea diving apparatus, and after we had crashed in our homemade plane during takeoff from the roof of the Muldoon barn, and after our submarine had failed to surface with us in the pond, but before Mr. Muldoon started being treated by old Doc Mosby for a mysterious nervous condition. I recall mentioning to Eddie that his father seemed to be awfully jumpy that summer, and Eddie said he had noticed it, too, and wondered if it might not be caused by eating vegetables.

Even as we sat on the fence, Mr. Muldoon came by on his tractor and stopped to study us suspiciously. "What are you two up to now?" he demanded.

"Nothin', Pa," Crazy Eddie said. "Just trying to think of something to do."

Mr. Muldoon shuddered. "Well, when you think of it, you let me know before you start to do it, you hear?"

"Sure, Pa," Eddie said. "I guess what we'll do is go dig in the dirt. We've been talkin' about doin' that."

"Okay," said Mr. Muldoon, shifting his tractor into gear. "Just don't build nothin'!" Then he drove off.

"What kind of hole are we going to dig?" I asked Eddie.

He stared off into space, his face enveloped in that dreamy expression that always accompanied one of his wondrous new ideas. "A big hole," he said. "A real big hole."

Digging the hole occupied us for most of a week. One of the problems with digging a big hole is that it is difficult to know when it is big enough and deep enough. There are basically two kinds of holes dug in the ground: (1) applied holes, such as for posts, wells, mines, etc., and (2) holes for holes' sake. Eddie and I were digging one of the latter. Eventually, the hole was so deep we could barely heave shovelfuls of dirt up over its sides. At that point, Eddie judged it to be finished.

Since Eddie had insisted that we keep the sides of the hole squared up, we had to pull ourselves out of it on a rope, one end of which was tied to a pile of stumps nearby. The stump pile also served to screen our digging activities from the view of Mr. Muldoon, who was cutting hay in a field on the far side of the farm. As Eddie often pointed out, any kind of engineering feat should be screened from the eyes of the engineer's parents. That way you could concentrate on your work and didn't have to be answering a lot of dumb questions all the time.

We were immensely proud of the hole, and I still don't believe I've ever seen a nicer one. It was so nice, in fact, that Eddie abandoned his view of it as purely an aesthetically pleasing hole and began trying to think of it as practical.

"You know what we could do with this hole?" he said. "We could make a wild animal trap out of it, you know, like Frank Buck does in Africa. We could cover it up with branches and leaves and grass, and wild animals would come along and fall into it. Then we could tame them and teach them to do tricks."

Eddie fairly glowed with enthusiasm as his idea began to take shape. "And then we could start our own circus," he went on. "We could charge people to see our animals do tricks. We might even get rich. Gosh, I bet we could catch a deer or an elk or a bear or a mountain lion or . . ."

"One of your father's cows," I put in.

Eddie's glow of enthusiasm faded. "Yeah," he said. "I never thought of that."

Both of us stood there silently for a moment, thinking of Mr. Muldoon staring down into the hole at one of his milk cows. It was unpleasant to think about.

"Tomorrow we'd better fill the hole back in," Eddie said.

"How about tonight? Maybe a cow will fall in tonight."

Eddie pondered this possibility for a moment. "I got it," he said. "There's a big ol' door out behind the barn. We'll drag that down here and put it over the hole." And that is what we did, before knocking off work for the day, secure in the knowledge that the door would save us from the uncomfortable experience of watching his father undergo one of his fits of hysteria.

Early the next morning, Eddie and I headed for the big hole, prepared to start the tedious task of undigging it. As we approached the excavation, a familiar odor reached our nostrils.

"Must be a skunk around here someplace," Eddie said.

"Maybe it's in the hole," I said.

"Couldn't be. We covered it with the door."

Nevertheless, the skunk was in the hole. He had apparently found an open space under the door, slipped in for a look around, and plummeted the eight feet or more to the bottom of the hole. Oddly, he did not seem to be frightened of us. Even stranger, for we did not know that skunks were great diggers, he had hollowed out a huge cavern under one side, in an attempt to dig his way out of the hole.

"We can't fill in the hole with the skunk in there," I said. "How are we going to get him out?"

"Maybe one of us could drop down in the hole, grab him real quick before he sprays, and then throw him out," Eddie said. "I'll yell real loud so he'll look at me and won't notice when you jump in and grab him and . . ."

"I don't like that idea," I said. "Think of something else."

"I got it!" Eddie exclaimed, snapping his fingers. "We'll go up to my dad's shop and build a ladder. Then we'll stick it down the hole and hide someplace while he climbs the ladder. A skunk should be able to figure out how to climb a ladder."

Eddie and I were working on the ladder when his father walked into the shop. "I thought I told you not to build anything," he growled. "What's that?"

"Just a skunk ladder," Crazy Eddie said.

"Oh," his father said. "Well, don't build nothin' else unless you tell me first."

Eddie and I went back out to the hole and stuck the ladder in it. The skunk showed no inclination to climb it, choosing instead to hide in the cavern it had hollowed out. Just then we heard Eddie's father yelling at us: "What did you mean, *skunk ladder?*" We peeked out around the stump pile, and there was Mr. Muldoon striding across the pasture toward us.

"Quick," said Eddie. "Help me put the door back over the hole!"

We threw the door over the top of the hole, neatly hiding it from view. Before we could think of a good explanation for a big pile of dirt out in a corner of the pasture, Mr. Muldoon charged up.

"Now what?" he cried. "Where did that dirt come from? What's my door doing out here?"

He reached down and grabbed the edge of the door.

"Stop, Pa, don't!" Eddie yelled, rushing forward.

From that point on, the actions of the parties involved all blurred together. It is difficult to recall the exact sequence of action, but I will try.

Mr. Muldoon grabbed the door and flipped it off the hole. Then he said, "Smells like a skun . . ." at which time he shot out of sight, leaving his straw hat suspended in the air for perhaps a quarter of a second. (Later, I deduced that Mr. Muldoon had stepped on the edge of the hole, beneath which the skunk had hollowed out its cavern.) A cloud of dust puffed up out of the hole when Mr. Muldoon hit the bottom. Then he yelled several serious swear words with the word "SKUNK!" mixed in with them. Next there were a lot of earthy scrabbling sounds, and Mr. Muldoon came clawing his way up the side of the hole, but the dirt gave way and he fell back in, saying something like "Ooofff!" It is important, perhaps, to realize that all the activity so far had taken place in a span of no more than four seconds. Eddie had meanwhile charged forward, yelling, "Pa, Pa, don't hurt him!" He was standing at the top of the ladder when the skunk rushed up that contrivance and emerged from the cloud of dust. Startled, and not wanting the skunk to reverse ends and spray him, Eddie grabbed the little animal by the head. The skunk started scratching and biting, so Eddie threw it back down in the hole, where its arrival was followed by a savage bellow from Mr. Muldoon, who, to our surprise, then came racing up the skunk ladder himself.

This was the signal for Eddie and me to start running, which we did, and we continued running until the thunderous sounds of Mr. Muldoon's clodhopper boots faded behind us, and still we ran on, finally outdistancing even the nostril-searing smell of Eddie's father.

Eddie eventually made his way home and placed himself under the protective custody of his mother, until Mr. Muldoon's rage subsided into the odd little facial tic that was to remain with him for several months.

In the ruckus at the skunk ladder, Eddie had been hit in the face with a slight charge of skunk spray. Worried at first that the spray might have affected his brain, Mr. and Mrs. Muldoon finally assumed there would be no lasting ill effects. Twenty years later, however, Crazy Eddie became a Ph.D. in chemistry.

How to Go *Splat!*

One of the most common activities engaged in by outdoorspersons is falling. Oddly enough, almost nothing has been written on the subject. It is not surprising, then, that few hunters and anglers know how to fall properly, or, if they do, how to score the fall on a scale of one to ten. The assumption is that any fall that results in a full-body cast automatically scores a ten. That is false. The full-body cast in and of itself rates only a five. Other factors must be taken into account, including overall style of the fall, the hunter's conduct before, during, and after the fall, and whether the fallee merely lies there groaning or manages to come up with a comically droll statement with which to describe his injuries. No one who fails to come up with a comically droll statement should ever have his fall rated as a ten.

I have been falling for years, in streams, over logs, out of boats and duck blinds, off horses and cliffs, and even from moving vehicles, to name but a few variations I have managed to work out. As a child, I was always falling. When I was five years old I fell out of a speeding bus. I can still remember my mother screaming as I bounced like a Super Ball along the icy roadway. "Not in your new snowsuit," she shrieked. "How many times do I have to tell you!"

Among my fishing and hunting companions, I am considered one of the world's leading experts on falling. They have become blasé about even my most spectacular plummets. Last summer I slipped on a mossy rock in a trout stream and shot over a small waterfall. My friend Retch Sweeney was so concerned he almost paused in his casting.

Unable to come up with a comically droll statement, I yelled at Retch, "Quick, get me to a doctor before this starts hurting! I've crushed my right thigh! It's a pulpy mess!"

Then I discovered the pulpy mess was a banana I'd stuffed into my pocket. Since medical science has not yet come up with a cure for smashed bananas, I told Retch to forget about calling the doctor, which he may have been thinking about doing as soon as he tied on a new fly and tested it. "Heck," I said, "I can fish with a crushed thigh. I'll just smear some banana on it to ease the pain."

The type of fall I hate most is the one-legger. This is where one leg shoots down a beaver hole or an empty posthole all the way up to the confluence of your anatomy. Your other leg is still running about up on the surface. The problem with the one-legger is that it lacks style. The person doing a one-legger almost always omits the comically droll comment and goes right to serious cussing. I recall the time my stepfather, Hank, did a one-legger down a beaver hole while we were fishing along a brushy bank of the creek. Hank had a talent for creative cussing, but the one-legger inspired him to heights that must have approached those of genius. He dredged up archaic curses from the distant past, combined them with current profanity, worked in a half-dozen anatomical references, embellished those with all the known vulgarities related to bodily functions, invented several new cusswords on the spot, and finally wove all these elements into a verbal tapestry brilliant in color and blinding in intensity. Hank never swore much afterwards, possibly because he knew he had achieved his ultimate in that field, or possibly because he was too occupied with his new hobby, which consisted of lurking about the beaver dam on the creek, baseball bat in hand.

The only fall more lacking in pure aesthetics than the one-legger is the pack-flip. This is where you're going down a steep grade with a heavy pack and suddenly stumble. This causes the pack to flip over your head, and the straps pick you up by the armpits, whip you over the top of the pack, and slam you down on the trail. Sometimes this sequence is repeated over and over, as with those little toys that walk down stairs: whip . . . SLAM! . . . whip . . . SLAM! . . . whip . . . SLAM! I once saw a guy who was packing out a hind-quarter of elk do a multiple pack-flip down a steep, rocky trail. By the time they were finished, the hindquarter of elk looked to be in better health than the hunter.

In regard to style, it is important to maintain proper facial expression during the duration of the fall. I prefer a look of casual disinterest, at least until I have plummeted past the ten-foot mark. Then I employ the standard grimace. The important thing to remember about the grimace is not to do it too long or too hard. Otherwise, the grimace may last longer than the injuries. I've known outdoorsmen who, three months after they had recovered from a fall, still looked as if they were about to hit.

What to say at the start of a fall is an important aspect of style. Many outdoorsmen are caught unprepared in this regard and have to resort to such clichés as "Yipe!" or "Yawp!" Therefore it is a good idea to prepare some appropriate comments well in advance of any falls you might take. Brevity, of course, should be striven for. The start of the fall is no time to launch into something like the Gettysburg Address. (Even worse would be to *finish* reciting the Gettysburg Address.) Something like "Geronimo-o-o-o-o!" is about right. Even that is too long for a minor fall and may be too complicated to remember under pressure. I have had it come out "Oronagiroooo" which sounds dumb and ruins the desired effect. "Oops" is a good one for any simple fall of less than ten feet, unless you happen to be still leading a packhorse, in which case you might wish to come up with something a little less frivolous.

Having established my expertise in regard to outdoor falls, I would now like to examine in detail one fall of which I am particularly proud. As I mentioned earlier, many outdoorsmen are not truly cognizant of the proper method for scoring falls. The following letter, from Gene Floyd of Walla Walla, Washington, is a case in point. I had accompanied Gene and his wife, Jane, and Bill Smith on a black-powder elk hunt last December, during which I attempted to instruct Bill in one of the advanced techniques of falling.

"Bill was impressed," Gene wrote, "with your falling-out-of-a-moving-truck trick, even though it was obviously your first attempt. He felt you did exceptionally well on the 'screams portion' but needed improvement on your form. Since you did display a somewhat individual style on overall performance, he scored you an eight. He briefly considered awarding you a nine but dismissed the thought when he recalled your arms were rotating like blades on a windmill, and definitely should have been kept neatly tucked to your sides."

I was shocked by the news that Bill had given me a mere eight. He is himself an experienced faller. Once, on an elk hunt, he stepped out onto an icy area being crossed by a large bull. Just as Bill was taking aim with his muzzleloader, the elk slipped on the ice and went down. While he was pondering whether it would be sportsmanlike to shoot an elk that had slipped on the ice, Bill's own feet slipped out from under him. He did a two-and-a-half gainer and landed on his back, firing the muzzleloader straight up in the air. "I figured the elk and I were even at that point," says Bill. He then jumped up, reloaded, and shot the elk. What I want to know, though, is whether it is sporting to shoot an elk that is laughing so hard at the hunter's antics that it can hardly walk, let alone run.

My first mistake was to accept an invitation to go on an elk hunt with this Walla Walla crowd. None of them knew the first thing about hunting etiquette as it applies to visiting writers. As Emily Post has pointed out, it is not polite for the hosts to walk straight up and down mountains without even making a pretense of breathing hard. The approach recommended by Emily is for the hosts to feign approximately the physical condition of the guest, which in this case would have consisted of sagging against trees, making strange rattling sounds with the throat, and occasionally stopping to scrape leaf mold and dried pine needles off the tongue.

But the important matters here are the fall from the moving vehicle and the method of scoring. It was decided at one point during the hunt that we should get into Gene's four-wheel-drive pickup and move higher up the mountain. We had already done this several times previously, with the four of us wedged tightly in the cab of the truck. I wouldn't have minded so much if I had been wedged against Jane, but Bill always managed to beat me to that position, and I ended up being wedged between him and the door. This time, however, Gene suggested that Bill and I sit on the open tailgate of the truck. The idea seemed sound enough at first, at least until the truck began clawing its way up a sixty-percent grade and over rocks the size of basketballs.

Since I was holding my muzzleloader in one hand, the only really good grip I had was with the other hand on a tailgate brace. Also, I was sitting on a little domed rivet head, and I got as good a grip on that as I could manage. I was doing all right until an ice chest in the truck broke loose and tried to ride me piggyback. The ice chest caused me to lose my grip on the rivet head, and I could feel myself slowly vibrating off the tailgate. Then Bill reached out a hand to steady me, or so I assumed.

"Better hand me your rifle," he said. "No sense in it getting all busted up in the fall, too."

I handed him my rifle, even as I turned over in my mind his use of the word "too."

Then I was gone. I executed a perfect three-bounce routine, including the difficult stunt of pressing one's nose between one's shoulder blades. I also managed to work into my routine the ice chest, which had followed me off the tailgate. If no rock of sufficient size was available for me to land on, I substituted the ice chest, a bit of creativity that Bill apparently overlooked in judging my fall.

When I regained my senses, I looked around for the truck, which I supposed would have stopped long enough to bury the body. But it was still clawing its way up the mountain, Bill perched on the tailgate, a rifle in each hand. I don't know why he didn't fall off, unless he was sitting on a larger rivet head than I had been.

As was reported to me later, when the truck finally reached the top of the mountain, Gene and Jane asked Bill where I was.

"Oh, he fell off about a quarter-mile down the mountain," Bill said.

"I heard he was pretty good at that," Gene said. "Did he get off a comically droll comment before he fell?"

"I'm not sure," Bill said. "Does 'Oronagiroooo!' mean anything to you?"

I finally figured out why Bill scored my fall a mere eight. He was going by the Walla Walla system of scoring, while I am accustomed to the North Idaho system. In the North Idaho system, we give points not only for screaming but for the originality of what is screamed. We also go in for arm-waving in a big way. I once fell off a high log over a stream and, by fanning both my arms and my legs, managed to suspend myself in midair for a few moments. I started off in a northeasterly direction, changed my mind and shifted to due north, and then set a course for the far bank. I probably would have made it, too, if I hadn't been losing altitude so fast. I scored the fall a perfect ten, even though it was several years before I thought of a droll comment sufficiently comical to fit the occasion.

The Human
Fuel Pump

Alphonse P. Finley and I were standing on his front porch discussing the desirability of field-testing his new snow blower on my driveway.

"No! No! No!" Finley cried. "I know how you are around machines! Machines don't like you. They stop and never run again. They fall to pieces and blow up and make strange noises! My lawn mower has gone 'punkity punkity punkity' ever since I loaned it to you last summer!"

"Nonsense," I replied. "That lawn mower went 'punkity punkity punkity' long before I borrowed it. Now be a good chap and get your new snow blower for me. You wouldn't want me to catch an infarction from shoveling my driveway, would you?"

"Hmmmm," Finley said. "Let me study on that for a minute. Hey, I got an idea. Maybe you could go down to the store and buy a new snow blower of your own. How about that?"

"Are you crazy?" I said. "You know I fish and hunt. I've got guns and rods I have to buy. I can't be wasting my money on snow blowers."

Just then a battered old four-wheel-drive pickup pulled up in front of my house.

"It's Retch Sweeney," I said. "I wonder where he got the new pickup."

"I would scarcely call it new," Finley snorted. Al doesn't care much for Retch and frequently refers to him by certain crude anatomical names. "I wonder what that elbow is up to now," he said.

Retch got out of the truck and walked toward us, beaming. "What do you think of my new truck?"

"It's beautiful," I said. "It looks as if it would go anywhere."

"Hmph," Finley said. "It looks as if it's already been there."

"Ah, it's just been broke in good," Retch said. "When I get done fixin' her up, this baby will climb trees if I want it to. First thing I'm gonna do is put a wench on the front bumper."

"You're going to put a *wench* on the front bumper?" Finley said. "That's certainly a novel idea. Why would you do that?"

"Why, to pull logs out of the woods with, and to drag the truck out of mud holes when it gets sunk in too deep."

"I see," Finley said. "You would need a pretty husky wench to perform those chores, I should think. Or perhaps you mean 'winch'?"

"Winch, wench, what's the difference?" Retch said, turning around to admire his truck.

"In your case, probably not all that much," Finley said.

"Still, I do rather like the idea of a wench riding around on your front bumper."

Retch was too excited by his new purchase to pay much attention to Finley's needling. He invited both Al and me to go for a ride with him. "We'll run her up into the mountains and try out the four-wheel drive on some really rough terrain."

I was a bit hesitant. One of the things I've learned over the years is that four-wheel-drives, like rubber rafts, will take a person into places he ought not to go. On the other hand, I couldn't disappoint Retch, and besides, I thought it might be fun. Finley, however, declined.

"First of all," he said, jerking a thumb at me, "it's against my better judgment to associate with him in an enterprise in which a mechanical apparatus of any kind is involved. McManus apparently is surrounded by a powerful magnetic field that does strange things to machinery, like making it go 'punkity punkity punkity.'"

"Now, stop exaggerating, Finley," I said. "Retch won't know you're joking."

"I am *not* joking! Besides, gentlemen, I am going to spend the rest of this cold, miserable afternoon curled up in front of the fire with a good book."

"It's all right, Finley, I understand," I said, patting him on the shoulder. "When I get old, that's how I'm going to spend my afternoons, too. Okay, let's go see what that truck of yours can do, Retch."

"Hold it!" shouted Finley. "I'm going!"

Much to his amazement, Finley enjoyed riding around in Retch's four-by-four. We took the truck up into the mountains, plowing easily along through foot-deep snow. Al had never been in the mountains right after a fresh snowfall, and was delighted with the beauty that surrounded us on all sides, the evergreens bundled up in coats of ermine, tall pines streaming with wedding veils of snow, creeks winding dark and shining through downy whiteness, and finally the mountains turning a delicate shade of pink in the pale light of the setting sun.

"This is marvelous!" Finley exclaimed.

"No kidding," Retch said. "And I ain't even put her into low gear yet. Now let me show you what this baby can really do."

"I was referring to the scenery," Finley said. "Wait! Stop! You're going off the road, you crazy kneecap!"

"Cool your jets," Retch said. "I'm just going to take her up this old skid trail and over the top of that knob."

"Knob!" shouted Finley. "That's no knob, you clavicle, that's a peak!"

Retch and I chuckled. Obviously, Finley had no idea what a four-wheel-drive vehicle was capable of. He continued to shout, whine, and screech as the truck growled its way up the side of the mountain. We wound in and out among the trees, climbed over rocks and logs, and eventually clawed our way to the top of the knob. By now it was nearly dark. The skid trail, if indeed it was a skid trail, dropped sharply down the other side.

"By gosh, I bet this ol' truck can handle that grade even in the snow," Retch said, gunning the truck over the top.

"No, no! It's too steep, you bellybutton!"

As for Finley, he was too paralyzed with fear even to speak.

Miraculously, the truck clung to the earth and, twisting and grunting, carried us along a narrow ledge with a drop-off to the right and an ice-covered cliff to the left. The floor of the cab was awash in cold sweat by the time we arrived safely at the bottom of the canyon.

"How about that!" Retch said.

"Mumph," Finley replied.

"Phimph," I added, discarding a handful of upholstery.

"One problem," Retch said.

"What's that?" I asked.

"It's too narrow to turn around down here. We're going to have to go back up the mountain in reverse."

Finley moaned cravenly. "I knew I should have stayed home and read a book by the fire. Now I'm down in the middle of a frozen canyon in the dark and there's no way to turn around and I'm in the company of two maniacs! This is the ultimate!"

Actually, it was not yet the ultimate, for at that moment the truck's engine began to make a peculiar sound.

"Huh," Retch said, his forehead wrinkling. "I never heard anything like that before. You ever hear an engine go 'punkity punkity punkity'?"

"Once or twice," I said.

"Ye gods!" cried Finley. "It's McManus's magnetic field at work!"

Then the engine stopped altogether. The three of us got out and raised the hood. Retch and I prodded and poked at the engine in the routine manner and with the standard absence of any hope of determining the cause of the malfunction, let alone of repairing it.

Suddenly, Retch snapped his fingers. "I know what it is! It's the fuel pump! The fuel pump is shot!"

"Phew!" I said. "I was really worried there for a minute."

"Yeah, me too," Retch said.

Finley stopped whimpering. "You mean it's okay? You can fix the fuel pump?"

"No, can't fix it," Retch said.

"Oh, you have a spare fuel pump then?"

Retch and I looked at Finley. "Sort of," we said in unison.

"Thank goodness," Finley said. "Look, I take back all the nasty things I said about you guys. I won't ever do that again."

"Promise?" I said.

Retch and I went into action. We quickly removed from the engine compartment the tubing and reservoir tank of the windshield-washing unit. This activity caused Finley a certain amount of puzzlement, but there was no time to explain. It was growing colder by the minute, and both Retch and I were aware of the dangers of hypothermia.

Once the window-washer tube and the reservoir were extracted, we used the tube to siphon gas from the truck's gas tank into the reservoir. While Retch was reattaching the tube to the reservoir, I removed the air-filter cover from the carburetor.

"The way it works," I explained to Finley, who was standing about rubbing his hands and stomping his feet, "is that we use the reservoir and tube to dribble gas directly into the carburetor."

"Ingenious!" cried Finley.

"Yes, it is, if I do say so myself," I said.

"But how do you fix it so just the right amount of gas is dribbled into the carburetor?" he asked.

Retch and I couldn't help but smile at the naïveté of the man.

"Well, it's like this," I said. "One of us has to sit on the fender, with his feet in the engine compartment, and hold

the tank in one hand and the tube in the other. Then he
squeezes the tube so just the right amount of gas goes into
the carburetor. It works like a charm."

"Oh," Finley said. "Well, which of you two is it to be?"

"I thought you might ask that, Al, ol' buddy," I said,
"but the problem is this, you see. Retch is the only one
capable of backing this rig up the side of the mountain and
working it along that narrow spot without getting us all
killed. And I'm too big to fit into the engine compartment,
bad as that makes me feel. That leaves you, Finley."

Possibly I have heard such wailing and gnashing of teeth
before, but I couldn't remember when. I asked Retch about
it, and he said he thought this was about the best wailing
and gnashing he'd ever heard, but he wished Finley would
get finished with it so we could start driving out of the canyon. A blizzard was in the making.

We showed Finley how to clamp one leg against the
wheel well down by the generator and to prop one foot
against the radiator cap so that leg wouldn't slip into the fan
and get chewed up. We warned him not to allow himself to
get bounced forward onto the battery, because battery acid
can eat the rear end right out of a pair of pants and usually
doesn't stop there. To his credit, Finley paid a good deal of
attention to all this advice. Finally we instructed him on how
to regulate the flow of gas into the carburetor, and at last
we were ready to make our run up out of the canyon.

Retch and I got in the cab, and an instant later the engine
roared to life. I shouted out the window to Finley and asked
if he was ready. He replied with a stream of crude anatomical
terms and something about a good book and a fire. I took
this as the signal he was as ready as he ever would be.

The truck tore backwards up the mountain, whining,

bellowing, and kicking logs and rocks in all directions. There was a good deal of strain on me, because I had to keep yelling out the window, "More gas, Finley! Less gas, Finley!" And so on. Since all I could see of Finley was his rear end, kind of pinched down on the fender, I could never be quite sure if he heard me or not. I thought the very least he could do was to shout back a reply of some kind, just so I would know he had heard. But that's the way Finley is—inconsiderate.

Scarcely twenty minutes later we backed onto the main road and were able to drive forward, with Retch leaning out his window so he could see around the open hood. He complained of the cold, and said he hoped Finley appreciated the suffering he was going through just to get him back to his warm fire. I said I doubted he would, because that just wasn't the kind of person Finley was—appreciative.

When we reached the highway and headed back to town, it occurred to us that we had driven over twenty miles on the mere two quarts of gas in the window-washer reservoir.

"You know what?" Retch said. "This is the best dang mileage I ever got with this truck."

"Maybe you should hire Finley to be your permanent fuel pump," I said, and we had a good chuckle over that little joke.

We didn't know that the gas in the reservoir had long ago been used up and that somewhere along the way the fuel pump had started functioning again. Finley had discarded the empty container, an unconscionable act of littering, and was now merely crouched under the hood trying to thaw his hands over the engine block. This no doubt surprised some oncoming motorists, or so we assumed from the erratic swerves the vehicles made as they passed. Many people have never seen a man crouched in the engine compartment of a truck speeding through a blizzard, and the few who have may choose not to believe it anyway.

Even the boys at Pete's Gas Station apparently had never before seen such a spectacle, judging from the way they gathered around and stared slack-jawed at Finley.

"D-don't anybody s-say anything," Al growled, "not a w-w-word!"

Someone commented later that the older Finley gets the more crotchety he becomes, and it's true. As I often tell him, he is indeed becoming old beyond his years. Otherwise, how explain his spending most of the following day in bed? Since Finley was too feeble to answer the door, his wife was kind enough to loan me his snow blower to clear my driveway. When I was almost finished, I noticed Finley glaring down at me from his upstairs bedroom window. I guess he had been awakened by the 'punkity punkity punkity' sound of his new snow blower. Old age tends to turn people into light sleepers, no question about it.

'Twas a Dark and Dreary Night

Back during my single-digit ages, I often thought about running away and joining the French Foreign Legion. The uniform was nice, and I liked the idea of riding horses and camels across the desert. Only one thing bothered me. I wondered if the Legionnaires were issued night lights. My love of adventure had its limits. I could easily imagine a battle-hardened Legionnaire sergeant reporting to his company commander, "Looks grim, sir. We've run out of food and water and the ammunition's nearly gone. Worse yet, we're short on fuel for the men's night lights." With my luck, I'd be the one whose night light ran out of fuel first.

I realized, of course, that fear of darkness was a serious flaw in my character. Since my character was riddled with flaws anyway, I didn't worry much about one more. Nevertheless, I didn't want my friends to find out I was afraid of the dark, and I went to great lengths to keep my secret from them. Take, for instance, the time Ronnie Ditmire came out to our farm to spend the night with me.

Ronnie had no sooner set foot in the house than he came up with the suggestion that he and I sleep out in the back-yard. He said he'd had a lot of experience sleeping out in backyards in town, but this was his first opportunity to do so in the country.

"Yeah, well," I said. "Sure. In the dark, you mean. Sleep out. That would be fun. You don't mind a lot of black widow spiders crawling all over you, do you, Ronnie?"

"You got black widow spiders in your yard?"

Patting my hair back down, I retracted a few premature goosebumps. Unfortunately, my evil sister, the Troll, over-heard our conversation and rushed to put in her oar and roil the waters. "What are you telling Ronnie? There are no black widow spiders in our yard, you silly!"

"There are too," I said nervously.

"Ma!" the Troll roared. "Are there any black widow spi-ders in the yard?"

Mom, ever ready to rush to my defense, stuck her head out of the kitchen. "No, of course not. Where did you ever get a dumb idea like that?"

"See?" the Troll said.

"I thought there were," I said, smiling weakly at Ronnie.

"Good," he said. "Then we can sleep out in the yard tonight, after all."

"I can't think of any reason why not," I said. "Unless you happen to be bothered by poisonous snakes. Ever seen anybody get snakebit? First they swell up into a great big horrible ball, and then they turn blue and green and yellow and then it starts to get real bad."

"My dad says there ain't any poisonous snakes around

here," Ronnie said. "So we don't have to worry about snakes."

"I thought we did," I said.

"Of course not," the Troll put in. "There aren't any poisonous snakes around here—not even when it's *dark!*" She cackled trollishly.

"Ma!" I yelled. "The Troll is bothering us. Tell her to leave us alone!"

"Don't refer to your sister as the Troll," my mother said. "Now, Trudy, get out of there and leave the boys alone."

The Troll backed slowly out of the room, grinning evilly. "Hope you have a good time sleeping out—in—the—dark. The weather report in the paper says there's going to be heavy darkness all night tonight *cackle cackle!*"

Just my luck—heavy darkness. And here was Ronnie, pressing ahead with his plan for sleeping out. This was getting out of hand. We were actually getting some old blankets and quilts down out of the attic to make a bed in the yard. What madness! I considered asking Ronnie to take an oath of secrecy and then confessing to him my disgusting fear of darkness. He would probably understand.

"I'll tell you something weird," Ronnie said. "I tried to get Fred Phelps to sleep out with me one night, and he said he couldn't, he was afraid of the dark. A big guy like Fred, you wouldn't expect him to be yellow-bellied chicken, would ya? He even made me take a secret oath not to tell anybody."

"Fred's dumb, too," I said. So much for that idea . . .

Darkness was already coming down off the mountain, crawling out of the woods, and oozing up from the creek bottom. Down in the swamp, a chorus of frogs welcomed the coming of night. Stupid frogs.

Several times in my young life, through some monumental miscalculation, I had been surprised by darkness while playing with friends at a neighboring farm. Galloping along at the head of a column of French Legionnaires, I would yell over my shoulder, "Watch out for an ambush, men. It's getting dark and . . ."

Whoa, hoss.

I take a look around. Hannnnnhhh! My deadly enemy, darkness, has slipped in between me and my house! "Uh-oh," I tell the other Legionnaires. "I'm late for supper." And then I fire myself into the darkness. I can feel its long, bony fingers clutching at me, its grisly jaws nipping at my heels, and I streak, *streak* I say, through the silent, creepy blackness until, at last, I burst into the benevolent, life-saving light of my kitchen. Startled by the bang and whoosh of my sudden arrival, the womenfolk emit small shrieks and bound about in a mist of hairpins. Ah! Once again I have defeated the enemy! I slide into my chair and ask, "What's for supper?"

The Troll detected my fear of darkness early on, and used it for her own amusement. Once, walking home with her through the woods in winter, I noticed that the shadows of the trees had lengthened and were now blending together into great patches of—darkness. The last of the daylight slid up the barren birches as if being sucked through giant straws into the gaping maw of night.

"It's getting dark!" I warned.

"So what?" the Troll said, crunching on ahead through the snow.

"We'd better run," I said. "We don't want to get caught out here after dark."

The Troll stopped, turned around, and studied me thoughtfully.

"We can't run," she said. "If we run, the wolves will attack."

I looked around, as one is wont to do after such an announcement. "What wolves?"

"The wolves that have been following us," she said. "Don't tell me you haven't seen them!"

Well, now that she mentioned it, I did indeed see the wolves, slipping along through the shadows to the left and right of us.

The Troll calmly studied my reaction. "Why are you twisting yourself all up like that, you silly?"

Apparently she had never before seen anybody wind up the mainspring. Not run! I would have laughed if I'd had the time and the inclination, but I had neither. *Sprannnnnnngg!* And I was gone.

At the time, I knew nothing about the infectious nature of panic. Otherwise I wouldn't have been so surprised when, upon reaching my top cruising speed, I noticed the Troll passing me on the left and still accelerating, her braids snapping like bullwhips as she cut in front of me. Maybe she thought there actually were some wolves following us, I don't know. More than likely it was simply that panic loves company. For my part, I couldn't have cared less about a mere pack of wolves. A pack of wolves wasn't even in the same league as a pack of darkness.

But now here were Ronnie and I, engaged in the insanity of actually spreading quilts and blankets on top of an old hay tarp in preparation for spending the night outdoors. If I even relaxed my feigned enthusiasm for the undertaking— good word that, undertaking—Ronnie would become suspicious. Then *both* Fred Phelps and I would become outcasts at school next fall, when Ronnie spread the word that we two yellow-bellied chickens were scared of the dark. Poor ol' Fred's reputation was already shot; mine hung in precarious balance.

Of course, all I needed was a tiny little night light. Something the size of a birthday-cake candle would do—a fifteen-foot birthday-cake candle. Any obvious night light, though, would cause Ronnie to put some tough questions to me, like, "What you doing with that flashlight and the big stack of batteries?" Even if I'd had a big stack of batteries, I couldn't have risked it.

"What say we turn in?" Ronnie asked. "It's already dark."

"I noticed," I said.

I glanced longingly up at our house, the lights of which were being flicked off one by one as my mother made her final rounds. She opened the back door and called out, "I'm going to bed now. You boys all right?"

"Yep," Ronnie said.

"Yaup," I said.

Mom went back inside, and minutes later the last light on our side of the house flicked off. Ronnie and I were in *TOTAL DARKNESS*! Not just the well-defined cube of darkness that filled a bedroom, but a great shapeless ocean of night!

"You ever hear the story about the stranger who got himself hung for claim-jumping, and his ghost still wanders these parts looking for revenge?" Ronnie said.

"Yeah, I heard it."

"Well, my pa seen that ghost crossing a field right out this way one night. Foggy it was, he said, and . . ."

Idea! Why hadn't I thought of it before! I leaped out of the covers and told Ronnie I'd be right back. "I forgot to brush my teeth," I said, rushing toward the house. In the bathroom, I jerked the string on the overhead light, waited an appropriate length of time, and then sauntered back outside. Perfect! The light from the bathroom window cast a nice rectangular patch of light right next to my side of the hay tarp.

"You left the bathroom light on," Ronnie said.

"Dang," I said. "If that doesn't beat all! Oh, well, a little light won't hurt anything."

"This ghost story is better if it's plumb dark," Ronnie said. "But anyway, this ghost . . ." He droned on about the ghost and its horrible doings. I smiled sleepily, starting to drift off as I secretly stroked the grassy patch of protective light, occasionally turning to admire it in all its loveliness.

Without warning, an ominous shadow suddenly appeared in my patch of light. Wha? I turned and looked up at the bathroom window. No! There, framed in the window, stood the Troll! She was in silhouette, so I couldn't see her face, but I knew she was grinning her evil grin as she stared down in my direction. Slowly her hand reached for the light string. NO! DON'T DO IT! She made several teasing motions with the light string, then— Zap! The light was gone. Faintly, off in the darkness, I could hear the hollow sound of trollish laughter. She would have already locked all the doors to the house. Trolls are nothing if not thorough.

So now there was nothing to do but suffer the night away. For me, the Troll had murdered any hope of sleep. Under my breath I put a curse on her: May a garter snake turn up in your underwear drawer! (And a garter snake would, which shows you can't discount the power of curses.)

A friendly wind swept back the clouds and a few stars appeared. Starlight was better than nothing. I noticed several little black shapes flitting about among the stars.

"And after the ghost got done with the two boys . . ." Ronnie was saying. "Hey, what are those black shapes flitting about among the stars?"

"Just some bats," I said.

"Bats!" cried Ronnie. "I can't stand bats! Quick, let's go inside!"

"Too late," I said. "The Troll has locked all the doors."

"Aaaaiiiiigh!" Ronnie said. "What'll we do?"

"I don't mind bats, myself," I said. "But if they scare you, maybe you can hide under the covers. Sometimes bats like to crawl under the covers, but if I see any try it, I'll drive them off." I studied the quivering lump under the blanket. "I'm going to be awake anyway."

Trailer Trials

Shortly after man invented the wheel, he invented the trailer. Ever since then, he has been trying to figure out how to hook up the lights.

I know a man who claims the lights on his boat trailer once worked twice consecutively. Anyone with one or more trailers will instantly recognize this as an outrageous claim, but the man is a member of the clergy, and for that reason alone I believe him. On the other hand, he's also a fisherman, so he may be exaggerating a bit. Possibly his trailer lights worked only once consecutively.

Over the course of his life, any sportsman worthy of the name will own a dozen or so trailers of various kinds—utility trailers, tent trailers, boat trailers, house trailers, horse trailers, trail-bike trailers, and snowmobile trailers, to name but a few. That is the reason researchers estimate that one-eighth of a sportsman's life is spent trying to hook up trailer lights.

The trailer comes equipped with a rectangular light,

whereas the plug on your car is round, or perhaps vice versa. In any case, you can be sure the two plugs won't match. Therefore you must replace the original trailer plug with one that matches the car's, a task that seems simple enough. You reason that since only four wires lead from the trailer plug and four wires lead from the car plug, there exist only a limited number of wrong combinations. True. The limited number is 4,389.

Once you have wired the new plug to your trailer and plugged it into the car plug, the standard procedure for checking the trailer lights consists of having your wife, Alice, if that is her name, stand behind the trailer and call out reports on what is happening to its lights. The dialogue goes something like this:

"I've got the left turn signal on, Alice. Is the trailer's left-turn signal blinking?"

"No."

"What's blinking?"

"Nothing's blinking. But the other light got real bright. Then it went out."

You switch a few wires around.

"I've got the brake lights on, Alice. Did the trailer brake light go on?"

"No. But the left-turn signal is blinking. Is that good?"

The check-out procedure continues throughout the day until it is too dark to work, Alice goes in the house and phones a divorce lawyer, or you are dragged off to an asylum. The divorce rate among trailer owners, by the way, is nine times that of the rest of the population.

Trailer lights have little insidious tricks they like to pull on you. For example, the left-turn signal will start blinking of its own accord. The drivers of the cars following you think you are about to turn left, of course, and thus are hesitant to pass. Noticing the line of cars stretching out behind, you drive slower to make it easier for them to pass. The other drivers think you are slowing down to make your turn, and they are now even more hesitant to pass. Eventually, some of them become irate. The others merely hope you will pull into the next rest stop so they will have the opportunity to beat you with tire irons. While hauling a trailer, I avoid rest stops.

Another little trick of trailer lights is to black out entirely, particularly on dark and stormy nights. The emergency procedure requires Alice to ride in the trailer and shine a flashlight to the rear. Since it is illegal for passengers to ride in trailers, however, she must be fitted out with a disguise. Wrapping her with a tent works fine, although there may be some difficulty explaining to a highway patrolman why a tent should be holding a flashlight and cursing.

Trailer hitches can be a problem, although they are nothing as compared with trailer lights. The hitch simply clamps down over a steel ball on the car. The steel balls come in three sizes—too large, too small, and just right. The just-right ball is the one you lent your neighbor to haul a trailer to Nova Scotia, because he had one of the other two sizes.

Once you have placed the hitch on the ball, you pull back a lever that activates a locking mechanism which always jams for a reason no one has ever been able to understand. Here's a tip. To clamp the hitch jaw against the ball, insert two fingers up between the jaw and the ball and then press down hard on the lever. The two fingers volunteered for this operation should be minor ones for which you have no immediate plans, or better yet, those of the neighbor who borrowed your just-right ball.

Trailers seldom come equipped with spare tires. Naturally, you assume you can purchase a spare. The trailer's wheels, you then discover, are of a size and style manufactured only by a small firm in Lower Tibia before the revolution. This creates the suspense of hauling a trailer without a spare tire for it. Getting a flat on a trailer without a spare rates as one of life's great predicaments. Your options are few. You can leave the trailer parked by the road to be plundered while you haul the flat to the nearest town to be repaired, or you can try to persuade Alice to run along holding up one side of the trailer, provided it is of the light-weight variety. If the latter course is chosen, I suggest you keep your speed at no more than five miles per hour and even slower on upgrades. Sure, driving that slow can be boring, but Alice deserves some consideration for doing her part.

Speaking of boredom, here's something guaranteed to relieve it. Going down a steep grade, you glance out the side window and notice some idiot trying to pass you on the wrong side. Then you see it is your trailer! Oh, it is a thrilling sight, I can tell you, especially if the trailer is carrying an eighteen-foot boat. Some people are thrilled right out of trailering. Others vow never again to try to get by with the too-small ball when only the just-right ball will do.

Safety chains, by the way, are required on all trailers. Their purpose, should the hitch come loose, is to rip the rear end off the towing vehicle, thus further punishing you for using the wrong ball.

I bought my first trailer a few years after getting my family started. Like any outdoorsman, I needed to haul stuff but couldn't afford a pickup truck in addition to the family sedan. The trailer served as a compromise.

A World War II surplus trailer, it was designed to be hauled behind a jeep. After much dickering, the proprietor of Grogan's War Surplus, Henry P. Grogan himself, finally threw up his hands in exasperation and sold me the trailer for practically nothing. It was a steal, the only one I ever got from the shrewd, tightfisted Grogan.

As a kid, I had distinguished myself as the most loyal and frequent customer of Grogan's War Surplus, which looked as if some minor battle of the war had been fought right in the store. It was a delirium of fantastic war stuff—helmets, fatigues, web belts, canteens, sleeping bags, guns, bayonets, machetes, rubber rafts, jungle hammocks, jerry cans, landing nets, and the like. During the years of my youth, I bought several of each item, with the exceptions of machine guns and tanks. Not that Grogan wouldn't have sold me machine guns and tanks if I'd had the cash. I was, after all, his favorite customer.

The war was long over now, and Grogan no longer prospered as he once had. The day I walked in looking for a trailer, I noticed him giving a customer the hard sell on a piece of merchandise.

"But what do I need a flamethrower for?" the man said.

"Why, it's good for all sorts of things," Grogan said. "Ridding your lawn of weeds, for example. You just go *whoosh* with this thing and the weeds is gone. Never come back, neither. You can burn out stumps with it, too, and let's see, ah, it works good for scaring off prowlers. Yessir, works real fine for that."

Grogan looked disappointed when the man walked out shaking his head, but he brightened at the sight of me.

"My gosh, boy, where you been? Haven't seen you in a year."

"Hi, Mr. Grogan. How's business?"

"Bad. But I expect it to pick up right away. What can I do for you, boy? Got anything you need burnt up real quick?"

"No, but I saw a rotten, rusty, old beaten-up trailer grown over with weeds in your back lot. How much do you want for it?"

Grogan scratched his chin stubble. "You must be referring to my little Sadie. That's what I calls the trailer, little Sadie. Got a sentimental attachment to her. How much was you figgerin' on spendin'? Not that I would let her go for any price."

"Twenty-five dollars."

"Twenty-five dollars! It cost me more than that to have a coat of rust put on her to protect the metal! No way you're gonna get that trailer for twenty-five dollars!"

Four years of college education gave me an edge over Grogan that I had lacked in the old days, when he constantly took advantage of me. At the end of some heated dickering, he finally gave in and sold me the trailer for not one penny over twenty-five dollars. It was a sweet deal, if I do say so myself.

When I got home, my wife could scarcely believe I had dickered Grogan out of the trailer for a mere twenty-five dollars.

"What's all that stuff in it?" she asked.

"Just a few helmets, bayonets, jerry cans, web belts, a landing net, and a few other things I bought from Grogan that might come in handy sometime. Now you take this contraption here—if we ever have a lawn and it needs some weeds burned out of it, this baby will do it!"

The first thing anyone does with a new used trailer is to paint it. Typically, the previous owner will have slapped a coat of leftover house paint on it, brown or white being the favorite colors. I would not degrade a trailer with such a paint job. I painted mine green and purple, but mostly purple, since the can of green paint was almost empty. It was not unattractive. The one green fender made it stand out from all the other purple trailers around.

"Let's go camping," I told my wife. "You go toss our camping gear in the trailer and I'll wire up some lights for it."

That night as I lay on my back under a sky ablaze with stars, I said to Bun, "Okay, now I'm touching the little green wire to the big red and white one. Which light goes on?"

Scarcely a week later, I had the lights working and we took off on the camping trip. As we wound up a narrow, winding road in the mountains, we entertained the kids by playing Twenty Questions.

"Is it a bicycle?" Kelly asked.

"Nope, not a bicycle," I said, chuckling.

"A wagon!" cried Shannon.

"Nope, not a wagon."

"A train!" yelled Peggy.

"Nope, not a train."

"A logging truck!" shouted my wife.

"Nope, not a . . . *LOGGING TRUCK*!"

By the time I had ground our old sedan into reverse, I could count the smashed bugs on the grill of the logging truck, a fate we seemed about to share. Expertly, I backed the trailer three hundred yards down the road to a wide spot, into which I swerved with several nifty little whips of the steering wheel.

"Good heavens, that was close," Bun said as the logging truck thundered past. "And to think, you've never even backed up a trailer before. Wow! That was wonderful!"

"Cut the sarcasm," I said, "and let's see if we can get the trailer out of the trunk."

I kept that first trailer for nearly thirty years, as kind of a memento of my introduction to trailering. It served me well, hauling my firewood, camping gear, rowboats, rubber rafts, and the fruit of my big-game hunting (usually apples, but occasionally pears, given me by sympathetic farmers). Last summer I finally offered to sell the trailer to a young man who needed it more than I. And for twenty-five dollars, too.

He tried to hide his appreciation. "Twenty-five bucks for a purple trailer with a green fender? You must be crazy, man. You should pay me twenty-five dollars just to be seen with it."

"Yeah," I said. "But it's still in great shape. Of course, the lights need a little work. Ever hook up trailer lights? Oh. Well, don't worry, you'll get the hang of it in no time."

"Gosh, I don't know," he said. "Maybe it is worth twenty-five dollars."

"Sure it is," I said. "And don't forget all the extra stuff I'm throwing in with it. See this thing here? You got any weeds in your lawn, pal, this baby will get rid of them fast."

The Grasshopper
Trap

Retch Sweeney and I were taking a lunch break from pheasant hunting, our backs propped against fenceposts on the edge of a stubble field. Suddenly, Retch's sandwich slipped from his fingers. Then he lunged forward onto his belly and began frantically slapping the ground with both hands. Had we purchased the sack lunches anyplace other than Greasy Gert's Gas 'n' Grub, I might not have been so alarmed.

"Quick, tell me!" I yelled at him. "Was it the ham-on-rye or the egg salad?"

Retch got slowly to his feet. "Dang! Missed him!"

"Who?" I said, wondering about the possible hallucinogenic effects of egg salad.

"A grasshopper," he said, picking up the sandwich and dusting it off. "Biggest dang grasshopper I've ever seen. The brookies up at the beaver pond wouldn't have been able to resist him."

"Oh," I said. "A grasshopper."

"Yeah. Hoppers are probably the best brookie bait there is. Too bad they're so hard to catch. You'd think somebody would invent a machine for catching them."

A grasshopper-catching machine! The mere mention of such a contraption drew me back into the mists of time.

"Oh, no!" Retch groaned. "I hate it when you get drawn back into the mists of time. I'm gonna take a nap."

The mists cleared. I was a boy again, running, lunging, and careening about our back pasture with Crazy Eddie Muldoon. The old woodsman Rancid Crabtree hunkered in the shade, shouting orders.

"Thar's a big'un landed on thet weed behind ya," Rancid yelled at me. "Gol-dang! You missed him. You got to be quick if yer gonna catch hoppers. Listen to what Ah'm tellin' ya now, or we's gonna be too late to do any fishin'. How many's you caught?"

"Six altogether," Crazy Eddie said. "But that's counting two that sneaked out of the jar when we were putting another one in."

"What we gonna do with three measly grasshoppers?" Rancid yelped. "You fellas jist ain't quick enough."

I held up the quart jar and peered in at the four measly grasshoppers. They stared back, their eyes filled with accusation.

"You'd think there'd be an easier way to catch hoppers," I said.

Crazy Eddie looked at me. "Say, I've got an idea!"

"Forget it," I said. Already that summer I'd had too many narrow escapes as the result of Eddie's ideas.

"But this is a great idea," he cried. "We can build a grasshopper trap!"

Rancid dismissed the idea with a wave of his hand. "Wouldn't work. Ain't no way you could make a trap small enough to clamp on to a hopper's foot."

"Not that kind of trap," Eddie said. He then went on to explain his idea to Rancid and me. It was dumb, probably the dumbest idea Eddie had ever had, and maybe even dangerous, if the completed contraption bore any resemblance to Crazy Eddie's other inventions. I was thankful that for once a mature adult was on hand to point out the risk and stupidity of such an idea.

"Sounds good to me," Rancid said. "Let's go over to maw place and build it."

Rancid's place, occupying a ragged clearing in the woods at the foot of Big Sandy Mountain, consisted of a pine-slab shack with a rusty stovepipe askew on the roof and various big-game skulls, antlers, and moldering hides decorating the exterior walls. It was not unattractive. A bullet hole in a window had been preserved as a memento of the time an offhand shot had been fired from inside the shack at a bobcat prowling among the junk cars in the yard, the sneaky beast no doubt intent on stealing one of the wrecks. Contributing to the overall aesthetic effect, ghosts of slain skunks haunted the air of the Crabtree estate, effluvial evidence of the owner's vocation of trapping. The odor of skunk, however, seemed but a gentle wafting fragrance to anyone working in close proximity to Rancid, a situation in which I soon found myself.

I struggled to hold in place a final piece of the grasshopper trap while the sweating old woodsman hovered above me, stretching and twisting strands of baling wire.

"Whew!" I gasped.

"Gettin' tard?"

"Nope. *Wheweee*! How much longer?"

"Jist about got her done. Thar!" Rancid stepped back, snapped his suspenders, and proudly surveyed the grasshopper trap. "Now ain't thet purty!"

"Super neat!" cried Crazy Eddie.

The grasshopper trap seemed to consist largely of baling wire, which held a legless chair to the right front fender of Rancid's old pickup truck. A gunnysack dangled limply from the end of a slender pole. A barrel hoop held the mouth of the sack open in the manner of an airport windsock. The pole was suspended with strands of baling wire from a superstructure of two-by-fours baling-wired to the chair.

"You see how it works?" Crazy Eddie asked me, apparently taking my silence to be the result of ignorance. "The pickup drives along a road and one of us sits in the chair and works the pole so that the gunnysack scoops up the grasshoppers from the weeds in the ditch. Get it? The guy in the chair . . ."

"I get it, I get it!"

The three of us climbed into the pickup and went rattling off in search of a good grasshopper road. From long experience, I knew that Crazy Eddie would try to persuade me to take the first turn in the chair. After his invention proved safe, as his inventions seldom did, he would then take his turn. But not this time!

Presently Eddie said, "I'll bet this grasshopper trap will catch a whole lot more grasshoppers than we can ever use."

"Ah bet it will too," Rancid said. "In fact, Ah bet Ah could sell the extras. Ah could build a pen outta wire screen to keep 'em in, and when a fisherman come along lookin' fer bait, Ah could jist net him out a dozen or so. Probably get a nickel apiece fer 'em. Hot dang, thet's a good idear! Ah might even git rich offen sellin' hoppers!"

"How about me?" Crazy Eddie said. "The grasshopper trap was my idea."

"And me?" I said. "I helped build it."

The great grasshopper magnate turned his shrewd, beady, capitalist's eyes on us. "We'll work something out," he said. "We'll work something out. Heh heh."

We soon arrived at a rough, narrow road that wound along Sand Creek. Hordes of grasshoppers crackled and sizzled among dry weeds in the ditch.

"Here's the spot," Rancid said. "Looks like the mother lode of hoppers. Now who's gonna be the fust one to try out the trap?"

I could feel Crazy Eddie studying me out of the corner of his right eye. "Gee, I don't know," he said. "It's sure gonna be a lot of fun, sittin' out there on the fender, watching those ol' hoppers pour into the trap." He paused to check the effect on me, which was nil. "Bouncing along out there, the wind blowing in your face. Be just like a carnival ride, I bet, and . . ."

"Say," Rancid said, "either of you two fellers know how to drive?"

Crazy Eddie and I looked at him. "Why, sure I do," Eddie said. "Of course, I'm not old enough to get my license yet."

"Hot dang!" Rancid said. "I'll try the hopper trap fust, just to test her out. And don't worry none about not havin' a license, Eddie. Thar ain't gonna be no policemen way out here in the dingles."

Rancid gave Crazy Eddie a quick lesson on some of the nuances of driving the old truck. "Jist stomp down on this here knob iffen you wants to go faster, or you can pull out this thang. Sometimes you got to pump up and down real fast on the brake pedal to get her to take hold. Now if she gits to jumpin' and jerkin' like she does sometimes, you can either do this or that. You know how to shift? Good."

Rancid got out and Crazy Eddie slid over behind the steering wheel. "One more thang," Rancid said. "Iffen Ah waves maw left hand, thet means go faster. Iffen Ah waves maw right, thet means go slower." He then squirmed through the network of baling wire and, with much grunting and groaning, got himself seated in the tight confines of the rickety chair.

"Let her rip!" he shouted.

Crazy Eddie stretched to peer up over the dashboard, while trying to reach the foot pedals on the floor. He pulled the gear shift down with a terrible grinding sound, and the truck lurched forward.

I was impressed. "Gosh, I didn't know you knew how to drive, Eddie."

Eddie's brow was furrowed in concentration as he wrestled the big steering wheel. "Well, it ain't like I ever actually drove before. I just know how. I've watched my pa do it hundreds of times. There ain't much to it."

To my surprise, the grasshopper trap worked wonderfully well. Eddie steered the truck along the edge of the road, while Rancid raked the weeds with the grasshopper trap. We could see the hoppers pouring into it.

Such was the initial success of the grasshopper trap that Rancid apparently decided he could easily double his profits by increasing the speed of the truck. Even though he was being bounced about a good deal, he waved his left hand.

Crazy Eddie ground the truck into a higher gear. "Would you pull out that thing there that makes the truck go faster?"

he said to me. "My leg's gettin' tired of pressing down on the gas knob."

I pulled out the thing on the dashboard. The truck leaped forward with a roar, sending Rancid's hat sailing away behind us. He hunched forward in the chair, his long hair streaming back. The grasshopper trap clipped madly along through the weeds, harvesting hoppers. Crazy Eddie's face beaded with sweat as he wrestled the steering wheel and strained to see over the dashboard.

"He's waving his left hand again," I said. "He wants you to go even faster." I couldn't believe the greed of the man.

"Okay," Eddie said, grinding into the next gear. "Pull that thing on the dashboard all the way out. Wow! I didn't know this old truck could go so fast! Now what's Rancid want?"

"Careful, Eddie, you're getting into the ditch on this side—watch out for those thorn apples!"

The thorn apples raked the side of the truck. We bounced over several large rocks, ricocheted off a tree, hit a culvert, and landed back on the road.

"Okay! Okay! Stop yellin'!" Crazy Eddie said. "I got her back on the road, didn't I?"

"Rancid's waving both hands now. What do you think that means?"

"I don't know. I wish he'd make up his mind. Maybe he's trying to signal we're coming to Deadman's Hill. Heck, I know that."

"It's all right," I yelled out the window to Rancid. "Eddie knows about the hill!"

"Now what's he trying to do?" Eddie said.

Rancid had turned into a large, bouncing blur on the right front fender. I could tell that his antics were getting on Eddie's nerves. "He's just showing off," I said. "But he'd better stop fooling around and sit back down in that chair, because we're coming to the hill. Oh, no! He let the grasshopper-trap pole get broken off! What's he thinking of?"

"If that don't beat all!" Eddie said. "Well, I guess we'll just have to stop."

"I thought you were going to stop, Eddie."

"I'm tryin' to! Now which one of these things did he say was the brake?"

We passed the sheriff's car going in the opposite direction halfway down the hill, but not by much. Even so, there wouldn't have been any problem if we hadn't been passing a wagonload of hay at the same time. The sheriff whipped his car around and came after us, red light flashing and siren wailing. As Eddie said later, it sort of scared him.

"What do you suppose he wants?" Eddie asked.

"Beats me," I said, tossing a bunch of hay out the window. "Maybe he's never seen a grasshopper trap before."

The truck stalled on the uphill grade on the other side of the Sand Creek bridge. The sheriff pulled in ahead of us and slid to a stop. We got out of the truck and walked over to find out what he wanted. The sheriff was grim and sweaty and looked tired.

"What you boys doin' drivin' that truck?" he growled.

Then he noticed Rancid, still perched in the tangle of baling wire on the fender. The grasshopper magnate was covered with dust, hay, weeds, and splattered bugs, some of which may have been grasshoppers. He had a comical expression on his face. I hoped he wasn't thinking about getting off one of his jokes, because the sheriff didn't seem to be in the mood for it.

"Crabtree?" the sheriff said. "Is that you?"

"Mawf fass phimpun grussheepers un . . ." Rancid sputtered.

"Watch your language, Crabtree!" the sheriff snapped. "Young boys are present!"

Crazy Eddie interrupted. "It's all real simple, Sheriff. You see, it's a grasshopper trap. Rancid's going to catch these grasshoppers with it and we'll put them in a pen and sell them for a nickel apiece and get rich and . . ."

The sheriff sagged. Wearily, he held up his hand for Eddie to stop.

"Please don't explain it to me, son," he said. "I don't want to hear."

The sheriff harangued Rancid for a couple of minutes and then drove off, shaking his head. Rancid raised a fist and shook it at Crazy Eddie. "Why didn't you slow down when Ah waved my right hand here?" he yelled.

" 'Cause that's your left," Eddie said.

"It is?" Rancid said. "Ah always thought it was maw right. You sure about thet?"

As we were driving home, I tried to cheer up the old woodsman. "Look at it this way, Rancid, at least we know the grasshopper trap works."

"Don't talk to me about it!"

I held up the grasshopper trap's gunnysack, which appeared to have been run over at least twice. "I think we might be able to use some of these grasshoppers to go fishing."

Rancid raised an eyebrow. "You mean some of them hoppers ain't squished?"

"Well, no, they're all squished," I said. "But we could make little balls of grasshopper paste and put them on our hooks."

At that moment I returned from the mists of time to the stubble field, where Retch Sweeney was just waking up from his nap. Retch blinked and yawned. "You ready to do some more huntin'?"

"Yeah," I said. "But first let me ask you something. Can you imagine a grown man going berserk just because someone suggested fishing with balls of grasshopper paste?"

Get Lost!

Several years ago I wrote what many experts consider the most authoritative work ever published on the topic of getting lost. The idea for the article germinated out of my observation that whereas millions of words have been written on how to survive when lost, absolutely nothing I had ever read dealt with the basic problem—how to get lost in the first place. What's the point of knowing how to survive if you don't know how to get lost?

Getting lost was a subject I knew firsthand. During my formative years, or approximately to age forty-five, I had deliberately contrived to discover all the various ways of getting lost, not only in the easy places, such as forests, mountains, and swamps, but also in less obvious terrain—vacant lots, shopping malls, parking garages, passenger trains, and tall buildings.

I discovered early in life that I had a natural talent for getting lost, a talent that through practice and discipline I honed to a sharp edge. By my mid-twenties I could set out for the corner grocery two blocks away from my house and, with practically no effort at all, end up several hours later in a trackless wasteland without the vaguest notion of how I had gotten there or how to get back. It reached the point where my wife would not allow me to go down to the basement to clean the furnace without map, compass, matches, and a three-day supply of food and water. I eventually compiled all my research on the subject of getting lost into an article entitled "The Modified Stationary Panic," which stands to this day, in the opinion of many, as the consummate work on the subject.

Although many scholars are satisfied to rest on their laurels, I am not. Several years passed without my becoming seriously lost even once, and I realized that I might lose the knack altogether, if I did not get out and do some fresh research. Thus, when my friends Vern and Gisela Schulze invited me along on a November deer-hunting trip in the snowy mountains north of their Idaho home, I quickly accepted.

The hunting trip started off in typical fashion. Vern assumed command and laid out the plans for the hunt, which included the admonition to me not to stray out of his sight. Vern and I have hunted, fished, and backpacked together ever since childhood, and I like to think that I have enriched his outdoor life immeasurably in providing him with countless hours of searching for me. Vern loves a good search.

Several opportunities to get lost offered themselves during the morning, but every time I thought to take advantage of them, either Vern or Gisela would come bounding out of the brush and herd me back to the trail. Then, about noon, I managed to give them the slip. I found a fresh set of deer tracks and followed them around the edge of a mountain—one of the best methods I've ever found for getting lost, and I highly recommend it. Soon the wind came up and snow began to fall, obliterating my own tracks so I couldn't retrace my trail, a nice bonus indeed! I can't begin to describe my elation upon suddenly stopping, peering around at the unfamiliar terrain, and discovering that I could still tell due north from my left elbow, but only because one of them itched.

I immediately began to perform the Modified Stationary Panic, which consists of running madly *in place*, whooping and hollering as the mood dictates. The panic will thus conclude in the same spot it began, rather than, say, in the next state. The Modified Stationary Panic, one of my own inventions, eliminates chances for serious injury, as often occurs in the Flat-Out Ricochet Panic, and also does away with the need for your rescuers to comb a four-county area in their search for you.

No sooner had I completed the panic than Vern showed up. I did my best to conceal my disappointment.

"I thought you were lost," he said.

"No," I said. "I was right here."

"Good," he said. "Maybe you've finally outgrown the tendency. Anyway, I just spotted the fresh tracks of a big buck going up over the mountain, and I'm going to see if I can find him. You swing around the north edge of the mountain till you come to an old logging road. You can't miss it. When you hit the logging road, follow it back to the car and I'll meet you there."

"Right," I said.

Ha! Vern's mind was going bad. Here he had just presented me with the classic formula for getting lost, and he didn't even realize it. "The old logging road you can't miss" is one of the great myths of hunting lore.

As darkness closed in, accompanied by an icy, wind-driven rain, I found myself scaling a precipice in the presumed direction of the mythical logging road. My spirits had long since ceased to soar and were now roosting gloomily in my hungry interior. About halfway up the side of the cliff, I paused to study a loose rock in my hand and recognized it as one that was supposed to be holding me to the side of the mountain. My plummet into space was sufficiently long to allow me time for reflection, although on nothing of great philosophical significance. My primary thought, in fact, consisted of the rudimentary, "Boy, this is going to *hurt!*"

Sorting myself out from a tangle of fallen trees at the bottom of the cliff, I took roll call of my various extremities, and found them present, with the exception of the right leg. Rebellious by nature, the leg now appeared to be absent without leave. Well, I could not have been more gratified. Not only was it getting dark and raining ice water, but I was incapacitated at the bottom of a canyon where no one would ever expect me to be. Even so, sensing that searchers might by luck find me too easily, I struggled upright on my remaining leg, broke off a dead tree limb for a crutch, and hobbled for another mile or so away from the beaten track. "Just let them find me now," I muttered to myself, struggling to restrain a smirk. "This is *lost*. This is real honest-to-goodness *lost*. It may be years before anyone finds me."

Detecting the onset of hypothermia, I built a fire to keep warm. But that is to put it too simply, too casually. No fire ever enjoyed such devoted attention. Cornea transplants are slapdash by comparison. The proceedings opened with a short religious service. Then pieces of tinder were recruited individually, trained, and assigned particular duties. Over the tinder I placed larger pieces, some approaching the size of toothpicks. At last the delicate structure was ready for the match. And another match. And still another match! I melted the snow from the area with a few appropriate remarks, and tried again to light the fire. This time it took. A feeble, wispy little blaze ate a piece of tinder, gagged, and nearly died. I gave it mouth-to-mouth resuscitation. It struggled back to life, sampled one of the toothpicks, found the morsel to its liking, and ate another. The flame leaped into the kindling. Soon the robust blaze devoured even the wet branches I fed to it, first by the handful and then by the armful. A mere bonfire would not do, I wanted an inferno. A person lost in winter knows no excess when it comes to his fire.

Next to the inferno, I built a lean-to with dead branches pried from the frozen ground. I roofed the lean-to with cedar boughs, and spread more boughs on the ground for a bed. Well satisfied with my woodcraft and survival technique, I stepped back to admire the camp. "Heck, I could survive here until spring," I said to myself. "Then again, maybe only three hours."

Once the lost person has his inferno going and his lean-to built, the next order of business is to think up witty remarks and dry comments with which to greet his rescuers. It's unprofessional to greet rescuers with stunned silence or, worse yet, to blurt out something like, "Good gosh almighty, I thought you'd never find me!" One must be cool, casual. Lying on the bed of boughs, next to the inferno, roasting one side of me and freezing the other, I tried to come up with some appropriate witticisms. "Dr. Livingstone, I presume," was one I thought rather good. Wishing to call attention to my successful fire-building technique, I thought I might try, "Did you bring the buns and wieners?" It is amazing how many witticisms you can think up while lying lost in the mountains. Two are about the limit.

I drifted off into fitful sleep, awakening from time to time to throw another log on the fire and check the darkness for Sasquatches. Suddenly, sometime after midnight, a voice thundering from the heavens jolted me awake. "Kneel! Kneel!" the voice roared.

So it has come to this, I thought. I stumbled to my feet and, wearing my lean-to about my shoulders, peered up into the darkness. A light was bouncing down the side of the canyon! And the voice called from above, "Neil! Neil! Have you found him?"

Within moments, Vern, Gisela, Neil, and the other members of the Boundary County Search and Rescue Team were gathered around me. It was a moving and dramatic scene, if I do say so myself. Calmly shucking off my lean-to, I tried to recall one of the witticisms I had thought up for the occasion. But the only one that came to mind was, "Good gosh almighty, I thought you'd never find me!" All things considered, that wasn't too bad.

Never Cry Snake!

I never have been particularly fond of snakes, but they have their uses. As a child, I used them to good effect in psychological studies I conducted on my older sister. The Troll, as she was known by me, was older and stronger than I, and won most of the skirmishes in the long sibling war we conducted over the years of my youth. Then I discovered her fear of snakes. By suddenly whipping a little garter snake out of my pocket I could stop one of her frontal assaults in mid-stride and send her into bellowing retreat. My mother once accused me of turning the Troll into a "nervous wreck." My feeling was that Herbie the snake and I had improved her reflexes by about three hundred percent.

In college, I discovered this same fear of snakes in my roommate, a nervous chap named Richard. (How nervous he was before becoming my roommate, I don't know, but he was certainly nervous afterwards.) I had become interested in the occult sciences by this time, and discovered that by placing a toy rubber snake beneath his sheets, I could induce Richard to levitate three feet straight up from the bottom bunk, where he would then cling like a possum to the springs of the top bunk. (I should point out that it is difficult to precipitate this reaction with a rubber snake unless the subject has first been conditioned by sudden and unexpected exposure to real snakes, such as might turn up in the subject's study desk.) Richard's screaming of vile epithets at me would bring Thorton, the senior who supervised our dorm hall, on the run. Thorton enjoyed an experiment in levitation as much as I did.

I ceased my levitation work on Richard right after my bedtime bowl of popcorn began to taste funny. "Eat some more," Richard would say. "How do you feel? Like a little more salt on it?" It then occurred to me that pharmaceutical majors are entirely unsuitable as subjects in scientific experiments, or so I deduced from the fact that my hair had begun to turn green.

My hunting partner Retch Sweeney, a tough, burly fellow, goes absolutely berserk at the mere mention of snakes, something that used to happen quite routinely when hunting was slow and I needed some amusement. As we walked through tall grass, I would suddenly turn, point at Retch's feet, and yell, "Snake!" He would instantly turn into a darting blur—a reaction that prompted me to nickname him "the Blur Darter."

Over the years, I refined this technique to the point where I needed only to point at the ground by Retch's feet and he would respond appropriately, bounding up into the air and darting about in a blur. Then one day while hunting chukars on the Snake River, of all places, I pointed suddenly at Retch's feet. He didn't bound into the air and dart about. "Snake!" I cried. He grinned at me.

"Ha!" he said.

It seemed scarcely less than miraculous. Perhaps through my diligent work with him, I had cured Retch of his abnormal fear of snakes, an amazing achievement for a person still in his twenties and whose only credential was a "D" in Psych 101. I tried to conceal my disappointment.

"You ain't never gonna scare me with snakes again," Retch said.

"Well, the least you can do is thank me," I said. "It wasn't easy for me to cure you. Furthermore, I did so at the cost of losing one of my favorite forms of entertainment."

"Wasn't you what done it," Retch said. "I took this workshop with a psychologist on how to get over fear of snakes. First we just looked at pictures of snakes. Then we looked at a stuffed snake. Finally we looked at live snakes. At the end of the workshop, I actually held a live snake! The doc showed us it was all in our minds."

"Gosh, that's really wonderful," I said. "Snake!"

Retch didn't blink an eye. "See? I'm cured."

We continued our hunt for that mythical bird, the chukar, but saw nary a one all day. Our faithful hunting dog had disappeared hours earlier and was now probably out on the highway, trying to hitch a ride back to town. The sun pounded us, insects gnawed us, stickers stuck us, but we pressed on. Working our way up a rocky canyon, we discovered it came to a dead end. A dilapidated corral sagged into the earth beneath a rock cliff. We leaned against the corral boards and studied the precipice.

"Looks like we got to turn back without any chukars," Retch said.

"Yeah," I said. "Wait! See that ledge over there? It's only about ten feet high at the low end. If you can boost me up onto that ledge, I can work my way up along the mountain and maybe I'll run some chukars down to you."

"Sounds good to me," Retch said. "Let's give it a try."

We walked over to the ledge, Retch crouched down, and I climbed onto his shoulders, leaning against the rock wall for balance. He handed me my shotgun.

"Ready?" he asked.

"Ready."

As Retch, grunting and complaining, slowly straightened up, my head rose above the brink of the ledge. I gasped. There, mere inches from my protruding eyeballs, lay a huge, coiled rattlesnake, ready to strike.

Speechless, I pushed back from the wall. Retch staggered about beneath me, his big hands clamping my feet to his shoulders.

"Sn-sn-sn . . . !" I said.

Retch slammed me back up against the cliff. "Stop fooling around and climb on up there!" he snarled. "You're not the lightest person in the world, you know."

"Sn-sn-snake!" I stammered.

"I said cut out the fooling around! That stupid 'snake' nonsense don't work on me no more! Now get on up there!"

He planted a hand beneath my rear and tried to boost me up onto the ledge with a mighty shove. "Ya gah gah aaaakkkh!" I said, unable to think of anything more intelligent. The rattler and I were nose to nose! And then I realized that the snake was dead.

Some insensitive lout who liked to scare people with snakes, realizing that this was the only spot possible to ascend the cliff, had coiled the dead rattler right at the brink of the ledge. I loathe people like that. In total disgust, I thrust out my shotgun barrel and swept the rattler off the ledge.

"It's just an old dried-up dead snake that some stupid jerk . . ." I never got to finish the sentence.

Retch cleared one side of the corral cleanly and took only the top board off the other side. He banked high on the rock wall as he roared around a narrow curve in the canyon, then accelerated flat out on the straight stretch. Six hundred yards later, he finally ran out of adrenaline and chugged to a stop, streaming sweat and gasping profanity. I let go of his hair and dropped from his shoulders to the ground.

"It was dead," I said. "The snake was dead!"

"I know that."

"So how come you went berserk?"

"Well, my mind knows there ain't no reason to be afraid of snakes, but my feet ain't learned it yet, that's how come! So don't let me catch you smirking. Another thing."

"What's that?"

"Don't never cry 'snake' again."

And I haven't.

Metamorphosis and Other Outdoor Phenomena Wives Don't Understand

I had done nothing peculiar. That's why I was somewhat surprised when Bun asked, "All right, what have you been up to?"

"Nothing," I said, innocently enough. "Why do you ask?"

"Because you haven't been acting peculiar lately. Every time you put on a show of being normal, I know you are up to something."

"Well, maybe I'm having a sordid affair with some beautiful and mysterious woman. Have you considered that?"

My little suggestion provoked quite a scene. It was easy to see why my wife might be jealous. Beautiful, mysterious women find it virtually impossible to resist handsome, debonair sportsmen. Nevertheless, I think it quite unladylike for a wife to display her jealousy by squealing with laughter and repeatedly slapping her thighs. In a fit of jealousy, a wife knows how to cut right to the quick.

"No," she said, wiping away tears of mirth, "I never

considered that. Now stop, no more jokes. My sides ache. Oh dear, but you do get off a good one from time to time. Seriously, I will tell you what I suspect. I suspect you sneaked a new gun into the house without telling me. Right?"

"Wrong! Wrong! I'll have you know I do not sneak new guns into the house."

"Oh, yeah? Then how come you have nearly twice as many guns now as you did three years ago? Explain that."

Here was a classic example of a wife's stumbling upon an outdoor phenomenon totally beyond her comprehension. Over the years I have noted many such phenomena. I have discussed the matter with other outdoorsmen and found to my dismay that my own experience in the matter is not unique but universal.

What had never occurred to Bun was that guns, confined in the limited space of a gun cabinet, breed and produce offspring. Just last summer I discovered a brand-new little Browning over/under 20-gauge shotgun in my gun cabinet. It was nestled right in between a 12-gauge Browning automatic and a 16-gauge Browning pump. I had no problem guessing what had happened. The gestation period of a new gun is exactly six months. I counted backward to the Christmas holidays, when the gun cabinet had been left unsupervised for a few days. Those rascals! No doubt they gave the Winchesters, Remingtons, and Marlins some ideas of their own. I thought about writing the Browning people to complain, but instead I'm raising the little 20-gauge just as if it were one of my own. The little devil has already gobbled up a case of shells, too.

Here's another example of outdoor phenomena that wives can't understand. A while back I told Bun I needed another boat. She agreed to listen calmly to my reasonable explanation, after I had pried her fingers from around my trachea.

"It's this way," I explained. "I have the big boat, right? Right. Then there's the rubber boat, which I couldn't do without. Sure, I have the two canoes, but I keep one only out of sentimental attachment. The other one is the work canoe. Of course, there's the duck boat. The rowboat? That's a toy for the kids. Now what I need is a simple little fishing boat—nothing fancy—that I can putter about the lakes in. Is that too much to ask? Here I work my fingers to the bones day after day trying to keep us afloat—uh, inapt metaphor there—financially secure, I meant to say, and you raise a fuss over my wanting a little ol' fishing boat."

"Oh, all right," Bun said. "I guess you can have a little ol' fishing boat if you want it. I do hope it comes with decent oarlocks. I hate the ones on the rowboat."

Oarlocks?

A few days later I brought the new boat home. When I showed it to Bun, she ran back into the house to climb a few walls. (We have one of those new phones where by pushing single buttons you can dial the police, the fire department, or the divorce lawyer.)

Eventually I managed to get her settled down long enough to explain the phenomenon to her. "Look," I said patiently, "this sort of thing happens to an outdoorsman all the time. He goes down to the marina to buy a little ol' fishing boat and finds about what he's looking for, a twelve-foot aluminum job with a little fifteen-horse kicker for power. So he dickers with the salesman a bit and they finally work out a deal. He starts to haul the boat home, but discovers it's grown to sixteen feet while he was dickering with the salesman. By the time he's three blocks from the marina, the boat's bigger than his car. He has to speed all the way home before the boat grows so big he can't tow it. That's nearly what happened here."

"Will it get any bigger?" Bun asked, gnawing a young elm by the porch.

"Nope, that's it. Twenty feet and three tons, with just enough room for two bass fishermen. It's so fast it's got an altimeter in it instead of a depth-finder."

"Well, if it makes you this happy, I suppose it's worth it," Bun said. "You are happy, aren't you?"

"Oh, sure. But I still need a little ol' fishing boat. Maybe I can pick one up . . ."

Have you ever had anyone try to run you through with a gnawed-off elm? No, I suppose not.

We now come to the problem of metamorphosis. (No, dummy, you can't catch it from a handful of leaves.) Metamorphosis refers to the transformation of a tadpole into a frog, a caterpillar into a butterfly, that sort of thing. You don't hear much about it because nobody can pronounce "metamorphosis." Even though you don't hear much about metamorphosis, there's a lot of it around, especially at our house.

Metamorphosis is one of those phenomena Bun just can't comprehend. For one of her many birthdays, I bought her one of those food processors, an expensive job. You could leave it home alone and it would have a six-course meal on the table when you got back. I wrapped it up in a nice package a few weeks before Bun's birthday and hid it in the back of a closet. That was my mistake. The closet was too warm, and metamorphosis occurred. By the time Bun opened her presents, the food processor had turned into a shotgun-shell reloader! It was one of those miracles of nature you hear so much about, the kind that leaves you sort of awe-struck and even a little reverent.

Metamorphosis occurs so often on her birthdays and at Christmas that Bun may be getting some slight grasp of this mystery of nature. Last December, for example, she hinted to me that she would like a really nice string of pearls for Christmas.

"No problem," I said.

"But they're too expensive," she said.

"No problem. I doubt they would cost a bit more than the neat little automatic I was looking at the other day."

"Well, you certainly don't need another pistol."

"Of course not."

The pearl necklace I bought set me back a sizable bundle, but I must admit it was lovely. Oddly enough, the box it came in was about the same size one might expect for a neat little automatic. Carelessly forgetting the possible consequences, I hid the package in the back of the same closet.

Christmas morning we let the children open their presents first, and then Bun and I opened ours. She unwrapped the pearl necklace last.

As usual, she seemed stunned. "You shouldn't have!" she yelped.

"Don't blame me," I said. "Blame old Mother Nature. She's the one responsible for metamorphosis."

"I mean they're much too expensive!" And she pulled out this beautiful string of pearls. She was right. They were much too expensive. If you can't trust Mother Nature, whom can you trust?, that's what I want to know.

"Dad's acting peculiar," one of the kids said.

"Good," Bun said. "It's nice to have him back to normal."

The Swamp

We had just been sprung from eighth grade for the summer. To celebrate, Birdy Thompson and I talked the old woodsman Rancid Crabtree into taking us fishing on Pack River. Rancid considered most of my friends "a bunch of smarty-pantses" but he liked Birdy, probably because of Birdy's having been born with a serious psychological defect—chronic gullibility. Birdy believed everything Rancid told him.

As we rattled along in Rancid's truck, the woodsman poured forth a stream of "facts" so strange they threatened to erode the very foundations of science. Through the mercy of time, I have forgotten most of the oddities of nature Rancid claimed to have observed firsthand "with maw own eyes," but I do recall the cross between a skunk and a porcupine.

"Now thar was a smug critter. Why, he could spit in a coyote's eye, and the coyote'd say, 'Scuse me, suh, fer gettin' maw eye in yer way.' "

Birdy was awash in awe. "Gee, Mr. Crabtree, I wish they taught interesting stuff like that in school."

"They should," Rancid responded. "But all them teachers knows is book-larnin'. They don't git out in the woods whar all the interestin' stuff is." Then he glared at me. "What you lookin' like thet fer?"

"No reason," I said. "I was just rolling my eyes, and they got stuck back in my head for a second."

Presently we came to the river. I had fished every inch of Pack River except for a section that meandered into a wild and swampy region. The river emerged from the swamp a dozen or so miles away, where it crossed under the road. I had never met anyone who had followed the river through the swamp, and it occurred to me that the fishing back in there might be fantastic.

"You ever hear of anybody who followed the river through the swamp?" I asked Rancid, interrupting his account of a tree-climbing rabbit.

"The only person Ah ever heard of to foller the river through the swamp is me. And Ah didn't have to hear 'cause it was me what done it."

"You never told me that."

"Waal, thar's a whole lot Ah ain't told you, mainly 'cause you don't pay attention to what Ah tries to teach ya. Now iffen you was more like Birdy here, instead of bein' such a smarty-pants, you might larn somethin'."

Birdy gave me one of his smug smiles. If there was one thing I couldn't stand, it was smug smiles from gullible guys like Birdy.

"Oh, yeah?" I said. "If you know so much about the swamp, Rancid, why don't we ever go back in there fishing?"

Rancid thought for a moment. "Thar's a lot of strange critters back in the swamp. Ah seed a killer bat the size of a goat in thar. Might of got me, too, 'cept Ah managed to git outta the swamp whilst it was still daylight. A feller shore wouldn't want to git caught back in thar after dark, Ah can tell you thet!"

"Sure," I said. "Listen, it's still early morning. Why don't we build a raft and float the river through the swamp? I bet we can catch some terrific fish."

"Ah ain't too hot fer the idear mawsef, what with the killer bat and all."

"Birdy," I said, "it's bad enough you believe everything Rancid says, but talking like him is too much."

"Sorry," Birdy said.

"What do you say, Rancid?" I said. "Let's build a raft and float the river through the swamp."

"Might be kinder fun," Rancid said. "Shore, let's do it! Ah got a saw and ax in the back of the truck. We can whup together a raft in no time."

Birdy looked wildly from me to Rancid. "But what about the killer bat, Mr. Crabtree?"

"Killer bat?" Rancid said. "Oh, the killer bat. Waal, we don't have to worry 'bout him lessen we gets caught in the swamp after dark. As Ah recollects, it only takes three or four hours to float down to the road. We'll be outta the swamp no later than noon."

Rancid's predictions had a way of sending chills down my spine. I didn't for an instant believe his story about the killer bat, but just on principle I didn't want to be caught out in the swamp after dark. It was still only about eight in the morning, however, and since Rancid's prediction had a margin of error of approximately eight hours of daylight, I knew there was no way we wouldn't be through the swamp by sundown.

Immediately after sundown, one of the first things I noticed about the swamp was that it had become excessively creepy. We had been lost for hours. The bleached skeletons of long-dead trees seemed to take on a ghostly glow in the fading light. Wispy strands of moss reached down for us like long gray fingers from the overhanging limbs. Darkness oozed into the swamp from all sides and began to close in on us. There was a stillness in the air, broken only by the sounds of water burbling against the raft, the splashes of our poles, and a strange, eerie moaning.

"For cripes sake, Birdy!" I said. "Would you stop your dang eerie moaning! It's getting on my nerves!"

"We're never gonna find our way out of here, I just know it!" Birdy whined.

"Go back to the eerie moaning," I said.

Rancid, seated on an apple box in the middle of the raft, scratched the stubble on his jaw thoughtfully. He had early on assumed the dual positions of captain and navigator of the craft, while Birdy and I did the poling.

"What are you thinking about, Rance?" I said, hoping he was about to come up with a brilliant idea that would lead us out of the swamp. Even at that young age I had discovered that when a group of people finds itself in a predicament, nothing so calms fears and nourishes hope as the expression of calm deliberation on the face of one of the members. It is an expression that conveys the message, "This mess we're in is but a riddle, which I am about to solve with my powers of inductive and deductive reasoning."

"C'mon, Rance," I said. "What are you thinking about? Have you figured out how to get us out of here?"

"Wha? What'd you say? Ah must hev drifted off thar fer a spell. You fellers got any idear whar in tarnation we is?"

Sometimes, of course, the person with the expression of calm deliberation on his face has the reasoning powers of a golfball.

Birdy raised his eerie moaning by two octaves. "We're gonna die in this stupid swamp, I just know it."

For the first time that day, I thought Birdy might have a point.

In its upper reaches, the river was an energetic, somewhat boisterous stream that flowed from one point to another in a no-nonsense manner. In the swamp, however, it turned lazy and slothful, sprawling out in a drunken stupor of aimlessly meandering channels. Most of the channels ended in bogs that could have slurped down a team of plow horses, had the plow horses been dumb enough to pole a raft into the swamp. Our problem was how to find the main channel.

Dark, shimmering clouds of mosquitoes and gnats hovered above us, kept at bay only by the periodic bursts of sizzling profanity from the old woodsman. As hoarseness overcame Rancid late in the day, however, the insects unleashed their pent-up fury and ravenous appetites upon us.

"Gol-dang," Rancid croaked through a haze of gnats. "Ah thank we oughtta go in the direction of that big dark shadow over thar."

"Which dark shadow?" I said.

"The great big'un. The one what's shaped like a barn."

Birdy and I started poling the raft toward the shadow shaped like a barn. Suddenly we detected some current in the water.

"Maybe we've hit the main channel!" I yelled.

"Ah told you Ah knew what Ah was doin'!" Rancid gloated.

We poled into the shadow, feeling our way through low-hanging branches. Dead moss hair brushed our faces, strange protuberances reached up for us from the watery depths. Then moonlight began filtering into the swamp. Mist rose from the water in a manner befitting a Count Dracula movie. Swamp creatures filled the night with eerie sounds—screeches, hoots, howls, chitters, chatters, and wails.

"Stop the wails, Birdy," I said. "They give me the creeps."

"S-say, Mr. Crabtree," Birdy said. "A-about where was it in the swamp you saw the killer bat as big as a goat?"

"Huh? What? Oh, the killer bat. Heh heh. Waal, Ah cain't rightly say whar it was. Might of been right near here. Area looks kinder familiar."

Birdy started with the wails again.

"Geez, Birdy," I said. "You'll believe anything anybody tells you. There's no such thing as a killer bat as big as a goat."

"Is too," Rancid said.

"Is not."

"Is."

"But M-Mr. Crabtree s-saw it," Birdy said.

"Thar! Thet proves it!" Rancid said. "And it was a fearsome-lookin' critter, Ah can tell you. Ah shore hope he don't notice us."

Rancid's mood had improved considerably, since it was now obvious we had found the main channel. Indeed, the water had stretched out into something vaguely resembling a river.

"Say, Rance," I said. "Let's make this ol' raft get up and move. Birdy's gettin' awfully tired. Why don't you take a turn at his pole?"

"Oh, all right," Rancid said, and the two of them exchanged places, Birdy almost instantly slumping into a slumber on the box in the middle of the raft.

We glided swiftly and smoothly along, the current now helping to carry the raft. It did seem to me that Rancid was working on a ratio of one stroke of his pole to every three of mine. In fact, sometimes there was such a long period between strokes of his pole that I suspected he was catching himself a quick snooze. It was during one of these periods that I noticed two Canada geese drifting on the water directly ahead. I expected them to take off at any second, but they too were apparently snoozing. Well, I thought, it will be interesting to see how close we can get to them. I knew both Rancid and Birdy would welcome the opportunity to see two wild geese close up, a wonderful bit of relief from the monotony of poling through the swamp.

The raft glided up beside the geese. When they were right next to Birdy—he could almost have reached out and touched them if he had been awake—they became aware that this strange floating thing going past consisted in part of three human beings. The geese exploded into the air over the raft with a thunderous beating of wings and deafening goose sounds.

"*The killer bat!*" screamed Birdy.

"Gol-dang a-mighty!" shouted Rancid, who obviously also thought it was the killer bat. He thrust at the geese with the ten-foot rafting pole as though it were a fencing sword.

"They're honkers!" I yelled, but in the excitement and confusion of the moment, this apparently was misinterpreted as "We're goners!"

"Not yet!" Rancid roared. "The bleep-of-a-bleep ain't got us yet!"

Then the geese were gone. Waves beat against some dark bank, but otherwise there was only silence in the swamp, and the sound of heavy breathing. The three of us stood on the raft, shaking. Even though I had known all along that the ruckus was caused by geese, the experience unnerved me. Birdy was momentarily paralyzed by fright, as I suppose anyone would be who thought he had just narrowly escaped the fangs of a giant bat. Rancid recovered much faster.

"Ah'm gettin' mighty tired of this gol-dang swamp," he said. "Sit down and gitcher selves a grip on somethin'."

He then poled us out of the swamp by himself. I remember the feat especially well, because it was the only time I've ridden on a log raft that achieved planing speeds.

Later, as the three of us walked up the road to get the truck, Rancid said, "You boys are dang lucky Ah was along. Warn't fer me fightin' 'em off, them killer geese might of got both of yuz."

"There ain't no such thing as killer geese," Birdy said.

I was astonished. Maybe the swamp had cured Birdy of gullibility.

Rancid walked on in silence for a moment, then said, "You know somethin', Birdy? If you're not careful, you could very easy become a smarty-pants just like somebody else Ah knows."

A Hunker Is Not
a Squat

One reason diplomats have so much trouble coming to any kind of agreement is that they sit in soft chairs around a large table with yellow pads in front of them to doodle on. They're too comfortable for serious negotiation. My theory is that world peace could be achieved in short order if the diplomats were made to hunker out in a barnyard and draw their proposals on the ground with sticks.

For hundreds of years, hunters have employed the hunker successfully in negotiating with farmers for permission to hunt their property. I myself am an expert hunkerer and would be willing to teach the technique free of charge to both Russian and American diplomats, just so we can get the present mess straightened out in a hurry. Most of my fishing and hunting buddies are skilled hunkerers too, and would be glad to help out. The diplomats, however, should let me know a week in advance if they want to attend my workshop in hunkering, so I can reserve a barnyard. I already have the sticks.

An ancient posture, the hunker was first employed by primitive man. He hunkered in the evenings by his campfire, watching simple little dramas played out by the dancing flames, although usually only reruns of previous campfires. During commercials, he picked moss from between his toes, having no bathroom or refrigerator to run off to. Then one night he discovered he could change the channel by poking a stick into the flames. During a particularly inane sitcom, he started doodling in the sand with the stick, and thus was born the classic hunker as we know it today.

Primitive man referred to the hunker only as "Ooo-ah," which may either have denoted the hunker or possibly have been only a natural response to the leg cramps associated with it. Even today I have heard men go "OOO—AH!" while attempting to rise from a long hunker. The word "hunker" probably derives from the early Scots word for haunches, which was "hunks." To sit down on one's haunches was, therefore, to hunker. Then, of course, it may not have derived from that at all, but who cares?

The hunker should be practiced at home until it is mastered and certainly before employing it to negotiate with a farmer in a barnyard. It is not uncommon for the unskilled hunkerer to settle down on his haunches, lose his balance, and then topple over on his back—fine and good on a shag carpet, but disastrous in a barnyard. True, farmers do get a good laugh out of seeing a hunter topple over on his back in a barnyard, but afterwards they are not about to trust him with a loaded gun out among the cows. It is the cows, after all, that make toppling over on one's back in a barnyard such a memorable experience. (The bill from the cleaners may contain a substantial surcharge and even a death threat.) I don't know why farmers insist on keeping cows, when they have all those pheasants and deer running around. I've talked to several of them about getting rid of the cows, but they won't listen to reason.

To hunker properly, bend your knees and slowly settle your rear down until it comes to rest just above your ankles. Your feet should be spread about eighteen inches, to prevent you from toppling over sideways, which is even worse than toppling over on your back. Your forearms should rest comfortably on your knees; if your belly is hanging out over your knees, however, you can rest your forearms on your belly, which isn't quite as good, but you have to rest your arms somewhere. Otherwise your hands drag in the barnyard. A barnyard ranks among the top three worst places in the world to drag your hands.

Now take your stick and— Oh, I forgot to mention the stick earlier. You always want to find your stick before you begin your hunker. If you don't find your stick first, you have to waddle around in your hunker looking for one. That makes you look ridiculous and causes the farmer to think maybe he can't trust you out among the cows. One of the main objects of the hunker is to impress on the farmer that you are a responsible person, and waddling about like a duck in his barnyard can blow your image all to heck.

Okay, let's say you are now hunkered and have your stick in hand. You want to use the stick to draw maps in the dirt to show the farmer how responsible and smart you are. While drawing the little maps, you explain to the farmer what you are drawing, because otherwise he will think you are just scratching up his barnyard. Don't go into too much detail with your drawing. Sketch in a few trees to indicate a woodlot, but don't try to do pines or oaks, say, because that will take all day and farmers are busy people. You should say something like this, as you point to the various lines:

"Now here's your north pasture, right, and you don't want me to hunt there because you have a hoard—uh *herd*—of cows up there. So, your woodlot is here and over here is your stubble field, where all your pheasants are. Those little dots there are the pheasants. I just want to hunt the little dots. What do you say?"

In hunkering with your farmer, you should be careful to draw him down with you into the hunker. You lose much of your persuasive power if you are hunkered and he is standing over you looking down and you have your neck bent way back in order to look up. This has happened to me on occasion, and I've found it to be quite embarrassing. Once, the farmer continued walking about the barnyard doing his chores and I had to waddle alongside of him, trying to draw quick little maps in the dirt every time he stopped to slop a hog or something.

Modern farming methods have complicated hunkering. Big corporate farmers now work in large steel-and-glass office buildings hundreds of miles from the actual farm. They milk the cows, slop the hogs, and shovel out the barn all by computer, and I can't say I blame them one darn bit. The farther you can get from either end of a cow or pig, so much the better, at least in my opinion. But getting a big corporate farmer to hunker right there in his office with secretaries running in and out can be a problem. Right away, for example, he wants to know why you're carrying a stick into his office.

If he offers you a chair by his desk, you're stuck and you might as well get right to the point: "May I get permission to hunt on your nine-million-acre farm out by Turnipville? I'll close the gate behind me." Under such circumstances, you've got about a ten-percent chance of getting permission. Draw him into a hunker, though, and you're already halfway through his gate.

You're in luck if the corporate farmer has a couch and easy chair off in one corner of his office. Plop down on one of those, which will force him to sit on the other, unless he wants the conversation to be carried on by shouting back and forth across the office. Next, reach the stick way out in front of you and draw a little imaginary circle on the carpet. (If you draw a real circle, that means you forgot to wash the stick after hunkering in a barnyard, and right then you can wave good-bye to getting permission to hunt.) Now, around the circle, sketch out the rest of the farm. As you do so, slowly slide off the couch or chair, whichever you've selected, and into your hunker. You need to do this with a smooth gliding motion, so as not to be obvious about it. Once you are securely hunkered, the farmer, if he has an ounce of true farm blood in him, should slide off his chair into his hunker. Right then you're as good as hunting the farm.

I once drew a corporate farmer into a hunker in the middle of his office by pointing out a tiny, intricate design on one of his Oriental rugs. He dropped into a hunker to examine it close up. Once we were hunkered, I switched the conversation to hunting and soon got permission to hunt. The man was an old-style farmer, though, and loved to hunker. He took my stick and began drawing on the rug himself, talking about shoats and goats and oats and other strange things. He had coffee and cookies served to us while we hunkered, and then we had cigars and brandy until at last I could bear it no longer and rose quaking and quivering to my feet. "OOO-AH!" I said.

"Pardon?" he said.

"Just another name for the hunker," I said, hobbling toward the door. "Thanks for letting me hunt the farm. I'll close the gate. OOO-AH! OOO-AH!"

The hunker is often mistaken for a squat, which is something entirely different. The squat has its uses, but it is an ugly posture, lacking in both grace and dignity. If you happen to catch a person in a squat, he is usually embarrassed and shows no inclination to engage in even small talk, let alone serious conversation. Seldom, in fact, do you ever find two people squatting together. If you inquired of a person's whereabouts and were told, "Oh, he's squatting out behind the barn," I doubt that you would have any inclination to go seek him out. I certainly wouldn't. On the other hand, if you're told, "Oh, he's hunkered out behind the barn," why, then you know the man is receptive to visitors and probably would enjoy a good chat about his lower forty, which is practically being eaten bare by the population of pheasants. The hunker is conducive to genial conversation. The squat, at best, may be conducive to some low-grade contemplation, but that's about it.

My first experience with the hunker as the ultimate posture for communication and persuasion occurred when I was about sixteen. Retch Sweeney and I enjoyed fishing the creek that ran through a farm belonging to Homer Poe, but we had avoided a particular stretch because it was too difficult to fish. The difficulty arose from the fact that Poe's house looked right down on this section of creek, and Poe had told us several times he would skin us alive if he ever caught us trying to catch his fish. We knew, of course, that he was exaggerating. The cantankerous old farmer would never even consider actually skinning us alive. He would undoubtedly kill us first.

The high risk of fishing the Poe farm added considerably to our enjoyment, and we should have been satisfied with that. Still, the unfished stretch of creek below the Poe house proved irresistible. At the first easing of darkness one morning, we sneaked onto the Poe farm and, concealed in brush, began casting out into the creek, all the while keeping an eye on the Poe house for any signs of life. Hauling out one huge brookie after another, we soon forgot all about the farmer and his dire threats.

Suddenly, Retch glanced up. "Poe!" he whispered.

Sure enough, there was the farmer striding down the trail from his house right toward us. Since he wasn't screaming and shaking his fist and in general behaving like an enraged lunatic, we guessed that he hadn't yet seen us. Walking behind him were the two gaunt timber wolves he kept as watchdogs. The dogs would run us down in no time if we attempted to flee.

"Quick," I whispered to Retch. "Let's hide in the old pumphouse."

Neither of us wanted to hide in the pumphouse, but it was our only chance to escape with our hides intact. Many years before we were born, or so legend had it, a man had hanged himself in the pumphouse. The possibility that his ghost might still be, uh, hanging about contributed nothing to the desirability of the pumphouse as a hiding place. Constructed of stone on the bank of the creek, it had grown over with some kind of creepy vine. Poe had installed an electric pump, but the old pipes dribbled water and the place smelled of mold and rot and dampness. Crawling through the cool, wet darkness, we shuddered at the ugly little scurrying sounds in the pumphouse and the cobwebs grabbing at us from all sides.

Just as I was about to convince myself that I didn't believe in ghosts, I felt a cold and clammy hand on the back of my neck.

"Hush!" Retch said. "You want old Poe to find us? I didn't mean to grab your neck. I thought it was a pipe."

We pressed ourselves against a wall, holding on to the icy-cold water pipes to steady ourselves. We hoped that whatever business Poe had down by the creek, he would get it taken care of quickly and we could make our escape undetected.

Then Poe jerked at the door of the pumphouse. His wolves began to growl. Had he seen us after all? I felt Retch stiffen as he pressed back into the stone wall. But Poe didn't come into the pumphouse. Instead he reached in with his long bony arm and began feeling around for the switch that turned on the pump. Obviously he didn't like entering the haunted pumphouse any more than we did, particularly if he could reach the switch from the door. Then all hell came loose. Poe screeched like a burst air hose. His dogs fled howling for home. Retch was whipped back and forth from one side of the pumphouse to the other. I thought the ghost had us all for sure. Wishing not to be outdone, I contributed what I could to the overall clamor.

Retch sprang through the door, with me running up his back. The wolves were now just black streaks going up the hill toward the Poe house. Poe was flailing about on the ground performing what looked like the Australian crawl on more-or-less dry land. Retch and I left him in a cloud of dust. Since we were covered from one end to the other with slimy cobwebs, he couldn't possibly have recognized us.

"I don't know what made me do it," Retch said later. "All I could see was Poe reaching for the switch, and before

I knew it I had grabbed him by the hand. He dang near tore off my arm before I thought to turn him loose."

After that, we didn't fish the Poe farm anymore. A person has just so much luck, and when you use up such a big dose of it all at once, you don't want to fritter away what's left just to catch a few fish.

A month or so after the great pumphouse scare, the old woodsman Rancid Crabtree asked me if I wanted to go with him to fish Homer Poe's creek.

"Not me," I said. "Poe darn near caught me the last time I sneaked onto his farm to fish."

"We ain't gonna sneak," Rancid said. "Ah'll jist ask him real nice-like iffen we can fish his crick."

"You mean you think Homer Poe is going to let us fish his crick just because you ask him real nice?"

"Shore. 'Course, Ah might have to hunker with him a spell."

And that's what he did. We drove over to Poe's and Rancid got out and confronted the old farmer in his barnyard. I could see Rancid's jaw working up and down and Poe shaking his head. Then Rancid picked up a little stick and sank down into his hunker and began drawing on the ground. Pretty soon Poe sank down into his hunker. After a bit, Poe began to laugh. I couldn't believe it. I thought Rancid must be drawing dirty pictures in the dirt, to make Poe laugh like that. After about an hour of hunkering, Rancid came back to the truck.

"Ooo-ah!" he said, rubbing his haunches. "That Poe is a tough man to hunker with, and purty dang strange, too. Ast me iffen Ah knew anythang about riddin' a pumphouse of ghosts, 'cause his garden is dryin' up fer lack of water. Now grab your fish pole and let's go fishin'."

The great thing about hunkering is that it has its own built-in time limit. A man can hunker for an hour, but after that his hunks begin to cramp and pretty soon he has a charley horse that could run in a steeplechase. When you enter into a hunker with another person, you know you have just so much time to conduct your business and you'd better get to it. That's one of the reasons I think we should get rid of those ridiculous seats at the United Nations and make all the diplomats hunker there on a dirt floor. Give the diplomats each a stick with which to draw in the dirt or otherwise wave at each other, and we'd get some of these world problems straightened out in no time. I can almost hear the debates now:

"Does the ambassador from the Soviet Union have any objections to the all-inclusive plan for world peace set forth by the ambassador from the United States?"

"Nyet! Nyet! OOO-AH! OOO-AH!"

Why Wives
on Christmas
Mourn

Christmas is nearly upon us, and once again I have neglected to patent my gifts-for-outdoorsmen inventions early enough to get them on the market. Next year! For now I will merely tantalize you with descriptions of the delights that lie in store for you next Christmas.

The Handy Dandy Hook-Remover—This item relieves anglers of the worst chore related to fishing. It weighs eighty pounds and consists of an air-cooled, gas-powered engine, an air compressor, a heavy-duty cutter, a gouger, and a ripper. No more will you have to suffer the frustrations of trying to remove hooks and lures from the plastic bubble-packages they are sold in.

The Exercise Machine for Outdoorsmen—My invention combines the major components of stationary bicycles, rowing machines, cross-country skiing machines, and weightlifting apparatus. The way it works is that you balance on a slick stainless-steel bar that simulates a peeled log.

Then a 150-pound weight drops onto your back, the steel bar begins to spin under your feet, and as you run to stay on top of it, plastic branches slap you in the face. When you are totally exhausted and begin to collapse, a lever is tripped that causes the machine to throw you against a far wall.

Deer and Elk Hauler—Numerous devices have been invented to help pack deer and elk out of the mountains, but almost all of them are cumbersome and still require considerable labor. My invention is simple, tiny enough to be carried in a pocket, and relieves you of all the strain of packing. It will sell for a measly $1.98, too. When the time comes for you and your companions to pack out a large game animal, you remove the hauler from your pocket and show it to your companions. It looks like an authentic pharmaceutical prescription bottle with the words HEART MEDICINE in type large enough to be read from ten feet away. Then all you have to say is, "Well, I'd better take a couple of my heart pills," and your share of the elk or deer will be packed out to the hunting vehicle as if by magic. It is important, though, that your hunting partners be compassionate and civilized persons. When I tested the "hauler" on my friend Retch Sweeney, he growled, "You better take the whole dang bottleful, 'cause I ain't packin' this elk outta here by myself!" Usually, however, you hunt with persons more considerate than Retch Sweeney, in which case the "hauler" works like a charm.

Fishing Computer—I have been working on a portable computer programmed to analyze fishing conditions, make recommendations on the most effective bait or lure to use, identify species, keep track of the number of fish caught, and weigh and measure them. I have based the program on my own vast knowledge of fishing. In effect, it will be just as if the fisherman had me at his side, offering expert advice. As soon as I can figure out why the computer keeps telling outrageous lies and reminiscing about the old days, I'll get it patented.

Thumb Protector—All outdoorsmen know the damage their thumbs suffer during an extended camping trip. The thumb protector is a hard plastic sleeve that fits over the thumb, enabling you to stir your cup of camp coffee in complete comfort and safety.

Automatic Fish Cleaner and Scaler—There are many useful devices on the market to assist in cleaning and scaling fish, but none so totally automatic as mine. Imagine, there you are, relaxing in camp, a cool drink in hand, while the automatic cleaner/scaler takes care of the day's catch! With proper adjustments, the only sound during the cleaning and scaling is a rhythmic humming. Now here's the amazing thing: the scaler will cost only $4.95! It is so small it can be used as a stocking-stuffer. In fact, the operative part of the device consists only of a small, shiny ball attached to the end of a string. As the directions explain, the ball is dangled in front of the eyes of your spouse while you chant, "Your eyelids are becoming heavy, heavy . . . you are now in a deep sleep . . . you love to clean and scale fish . . . you will hum rhythmically while cleaning and scaling fish . . ."

Canary in a Cage—This is a safety device to be employed in any tent or cabin occupied by more than two hunters after the third day of a hunt. When the canary topples from its perch and strikes a bell, the alarm warns hunters that the air has become lethal. The canary can also be used to test individual hunters as they enter the shelter. Merely sweep the cage over the subject, much as you would use a Geiger counter in checking radiation levels. If the canary wobbles on its perch, coughs, or chokes, the offending individual should be forced to sleep outside. Replacement canaries are available for $29.95.

The Complete Float Tube—As you know, the standard float tube requires that you paddle it about with rubber flippers on your feet. The Complete Float Tube, however, is equipped with a one-horse outboard motor. But, you ask, won't your feet get caught in the prop? After my product tester, Fred "Stubby" Phipps, complained about just that very problem, we enclosed the prop in a wire-mesh cage, which solved the difficulty. The CPT also comes with a sail. So far we have had only one opportunity to test the sail, and that was on Puget Sound during a nasty storm. The only problem we detected with the sail was that it hung up on the mast, preventing its being lowered. I will get that little bug worked out as soon as Stubby returns. He was last seen off the Aleutian Islands doing about twenty knots, which isn't bad for a float tube.

Sleeping-Bag Shucker—Every outdoorsman knows how difficult it is to shuck his companions out of their sleeping bags on cold mornings, particularly when it is their turn to build the fire. The Shucker can now take over this difficult chore. It consists of a large inflatable bear, which you blow up and place next to your companion after he has gone to sleep. The next morning, all you need do is yell "Bear in tent!" to shuck the person out of his sleeping bag. This obviously is a great improvement over my previous design for a sleeping-bag shucker, which required you to get up, insert the bottom of your companion's bag between the rollers, and crank it through.

Anti-Purist Fly Box—Here is the perfect gift for you if you must associate with fly-fishing purists. It appears to be a standard fly box, but when a secret button is pressed, a panel slides open to reveal a matched set of night crawlers.

Well, that's enough Christmas delights to tantalize you with. Now, I have to go clean the basement. I love cleaning the basement. Before my wife found out how to work the Automatic Fish Cleaner and Scaler, I didn't care that much for cleaning the basement. Hmmm. Hmmm. Hmmmm.

The Hunting Lesson

Over the years it has been my distinct honor and pleasure to introduce numerous persons to the sport of hunting. It is odd, however, that a man can have a thousand successes and one failure, and it will be the failure that sticks in his mind like a porky quill in a hound's nose. Thus it is with my single failure, one Sidney Sample. Even now, five years later, I torment myself with the question of where I went wrong. How did I slip with Sample?

The affair started off innocently enough. One fall day, with none of my regular hunting partners available for the following weekend, I strolled next door to Sidney's house to invite him to go deer hunting with me. I found him digging up bulbs in the garden, and greeted him informally, namely by sneaking up behind him and dumping a basket of moldering leaves over his head. Not one to enjoy a good joke on himself, Sidney growled malevolently and thrust blindly at me with the garden trowel.

"Sidney," I said, holding him at bay with a rake handle, "I am about to give you the opportunity of a lifetime. How would you like to go deer hunting with me?"

"Not much," he replied, fingering leaf mold from his ears. "In fact, my desire to go hunting with you is so slight as to escape detection by modern science!"

"Don't like hunting, huh?" I said. "Well, many people who have never been exposed to the sport feel that way about it. Listen, I can teach you all about hunting. One weekend out with me, and you'll come back loving it."

"No," Sidney snarled.

"If nothing else, you'll enjoy getting out in the crisp mountain air. It will invigorate you."

"No! No! *NO!*"

"Sid, I just know you'll enjoy the camaraderie of the hunting camp, the thrill of the pursuit, the . . ."

"No, I tell you, no! *Go home!*"

". . . the free meat and . . ."

"Free meat?"

"Sure. Just think of packing away all those free venison steaks and chops and roasts in the freezer."

"Free meat. Venison's good, too. I tasted it once. Yeah, I wouldn't mind getting a bunch of free meat. Then, too, as you say, there's the hunting-camp camaraderie, the crisp mountain air, and the thrill of pursuit. But I'm willing to put up with all that stuff if I can get some free meat."

I would have patted him on the shoulder, but I didn't want to get my hands all dirty with leaf mold. "I can see right now you have the makings of a true sportsman," I told him.

"So how do I get this free deer?" Sidney asked.

"Well, you just go out with me and get it. Of course,

there are a few odds and ends you'll need to pick up down at Duffy's Sporting Goods."

"Like what?"

"Oh, let's see. You'll need a rifle, of course. Outfitted with scope and sling. A couple boxes of shells. Seems to me there's something else. A knife! You'll need a good hunting knife. And a whetstone. I nearly forgot the whetstone. That should be about it. You have a good pair of insulated boots, don't you? No? Oh, wool pants, you'll need wool pants and some good wool socks and a wool shirt and a down parka and some thermal underwear and an orange hunting vest and a red cap. Heck, that should do it. Good, you're making a list. Did I say gloves? Get some gloves. Oh, binoculars! And a first-aid kit. And a survival kit, with a daypack to carry it in. Rope, you'll need a length of rope for dragging your free deer out of the mountains with. We could use my tent, of course, but it has a rip in the roof on the guest's side. You might want to buy a tent. A subzero sleeping bag, did I mention that? You'll probably want an insulated sleeping pad, too. Down booties are awfully nice to slip into when you take off your hunting boots, but they're optional. Then there's the grub, and that's it. Did I mention the hunting license and deer tag?"

"Hmmmm," Sidney said, studying his list. "Just how big are these free deer, anyway?"

"Big!" I said. "Real big!"

"Geez," he said, "I don't know how I can afford to buy all the stuff on this list."

"Take some advice from an old experienced hunter— mortgage the house."

After Sidney purchased his outfit, I took him out to the gun-club range and we sighted in his rifle. He grouped his last five shots right in the center of the bull's-eye. Then I showed him my technique of scattering shots randomly around the target because, as I explained, you never know which way the deer might jump just as you pull the trigger.

"How long before I learn to do that?" Sidney asked.

"Years," I said. "It's not something you master overnight."

The day before the hunt, Retch Sweeney called up and said he would be able to go hunting after all.

"How come he's going?" Sidney snapped when I told him the news. They are not exactly bosom buddies.

"He's between jobs," I said.

"I didn't know he ever worked," Sidney growled. "When did he get laid off?"

"Nineteen fifty-seven."

I explained to Sidney the absolute necessity of being ready when Retch and I came to pick him up the next morning. "We'll arrive at your house at two sharp. Got that? *Two sharp!*"

"Right," he said.

"Don't bother about breakfast. We can grab a quick bite at Greasy Gert's Gas 'n' Grub just before we turn off the highway and head up to our hunting area. Now remember, *two sharp!*"

We picked Sidney up the next morning at exactly 5:35. He was furious. Naturally, Retch and I were puzzled. Then it occurred to me that since this was Sidney's first hunt, he didn't realize that when hunters say "two sharp," they mean "sometime around five."

"Stop whimpering and toss your gear in back," Retch said. "You better not have forgot nothin' either, because we're not turnin' around and comin' back for it! Now put your rifle in the rack next to mine."

"What do you mean, next to yours?"

"That ol' .30-06 right there . . . Say, I wonder if you fellas would mind swingin' by my house again. Just take a few minutes."

After Retch had picked up his rifle and I had returned to my house for my sleeping bag and then we had gone back to Retch's for his shells, it was almost six-thirty by the time we got out to the highway.

"Aren't we going to be awfully late with all these delays?" Sidney asked. "What time will we start hunting?"

Retch and I looked at each other and laughed. "Why, man, we're already hunting!" Retch said. "This is it. This is what hunting's all about."

We drove along for an hour, as Retch and I entertained Sidney with detailed accounts of other hunting trips. "It was a tough shot, looked impossible to me at first," Retch was saying. "That six-point buck was going away from me at an angle and . . ."

I held up my hand for silence. "Okay, now we got to get serious. We're coming to the most dangerous part of the trip. We get through this ordeal and we should be okay. You guys watch yourselves. If you start to feel faint or queasy, Sid, let me know right away."

"Cripes!" Sidney said nervously. "What do we have to do, drive up a sheer cliff or something?"

"Worse," I said. "We're going to eat breakfast at Greasy Gert's."

Dawn had long since cracked and spilled over the mountains by the time we arrived at our hunting spot. Retch looked out the window and groaned.

"What are you groaning for?" I asked. "I'm the one that had Gerty's chili-pepper omelette."

"It's not that," Retch said. "I see fresh tracks in the snow all over the place. If we'd been here an hour earlier, we'd have nailed us some deer."

"Listen," I said. "Did we come out to nail deer or to go hunting today? If we're hunting, we have to get up two hours late, forget a bunch of stuff we have to go back for, and then stop for breakfast at Gerty's. You know how it's done."

"Yeah, sorry, I forgot for a second when I saw the tracks," Retch said. "I got carried away. Who cares about nailing deer right off!"

"I do!" Sidney yelped. "I just bought twenty-five hundred dollars worth of hunting stuff, and I want to get my free deer!"

It was clear that Sidney had a lot to learn about hunting, so I lost no time in starting on his first lesson. I put him on a stand and told him that Retch and I would sweep around the far side of the ridge and drive some deer past him. "We'll be back in an hour," I told him. "Don't move!"

Retch and I returned three hours later and found Sidney still on the stand. He was frosted over and stiff as an icicle. We leaned him against a tree until we got a fire going to thaw him out.

"How come you didn't move around?" I asked him.

"Y-you t-told me to stay on the st-stand. You said y-you would be b-back in an hour, and for me not to m-move."

"I'm sorry, I should have explained," I said. "When a hunter says he'll be back in an hour, that means not less than three hours. Furthermore, nobody ever stays on a stand as he's told to. As soon as the other hunters are out of sight, he beats it off to some other place where he's sure there's a deer but there never is. That's standard procedure. I guess I should have mentioned it to you."

"Yeah," Retch said. "Anyway, next time you'll know. It

takes a while to catch on to deer hunting. Well, we might as well make camp. We ain't gonna get no deer today."

"Oh, I got one!" Sidney said. "See, he's lying over there behind that log. He was too big for me to move by myself. Right after you fellows left, he came tearing along the trail there, and I shot him."

"Oh-oh!" I said. "Better go have a look, Retch."

Retch walked over to the deer, looked down, shook his head, and walked back.

"We're in for it now," he told me.

"How bad is it?" I asked.

"Six points."

"Cripes!" I said.

"Did I do it wrong?" Sidney asked.

"We'll have to wait and see," I said.

Sidney thought for a moment, then smiled. "Gee, wouldn't it be funny if I was the only one to get a deer and it was my first trip and all, and you guys were teaching me how to hunt. Not that I would ever mention it to the guys down at Kelly's Bar & Grill, but . . . Is six points good? Say, let me tell you how I got him. It was a tough shot, looked impossible to me at first. The six-point buck was going away from me at an angle, and . . ."

"It's going to be even worse than I first thought," Retch said.

"Yeah," I said. "Ol' Sidney learns fast. Well, you can't win 'em all."

First Knife

In the time of my youth, the eighth birthday was special because that was the one at which your first pocketknife was bestowed upon you. Seven-year-olds were considered too immature and irresponsible to carry knives. Only when you turned eight did you grasp the absolute wisdom of this parental policy. It suddenly became quite obvious that the only reason God had made seven-year-olds at all was to heighten the satisfaction of eight-year-olds in owning a pocketknife.

"C'mon, lemme whittle with your knife, Jack," a seven-year-old brother would beg.

"Sorry, Willy, I can't do it," the eight-year-old would respond maturely. "You're too little."

"But, Jack, you cut *yourself*!"

"Yeah, but I'm bigger, see. I got more blood. I can spare the blood."

When parents made the presentation of the pocketknife,

they always warned the kid, "Now don't cut yourself!" For some reason it was generally assumed that cutting himself was high on the kid's list of priorities.

The kid did four things with his new knife. First, he whittled a stick. Second, he cut himself. Third, he sharpened the knife. Fourth, he lost it. All four activities occurred within approximately twenty-four hours after the knife was presented to him. Many authorities on the subject believe that the fourth thing the kid did with his first knife was to break the point off the big blade trying to pry the cap off a bottle of pop, but they are wrong. That always happened to the second knife. The first knife was never around long enough for the kid to think of prying a pop-bottle cap off with it.

Let's consider in more detail the four applications of the first knife during its brief history.

Whittling—You would select a straight-grained piece of cedar from the kindling box and reduce it to a pile of shavings. These shavings would then take on a life of their own, migrating to the sofa, your mother's favorite rug, and the linen closet. They would turn up on your father's new suit and your sister's party dress. It was not unusual to find one sailing across a bowl of gravy during supper. The shavings seemed to reproduce themselves. After being freed from the stick, they went forth and multiplied. Parental threats against your person also multiplied, and you would from time to time hear muttered accusations exchanged between mother and father about whose idea it was to give you a knife anyway. Still, there was no turning back. Once you had whittled, you had the need always to whittle.

Cutting Yourself—Cuts were not distributed randomly about your body, as many mothers feared and predicted. They were almost always confined to the section between the first and second knuckles on the index finger of the hand opposite the one that held the knife. Usually the first knife was only around long enough to produce one cut. This cut came as a great surprise and was never the result of carelessness but of some extraordinary circumstance. "A gust of wind blew my hand," you would tell your mother. As she applied the bandage, she would wonder aloud if the blood-stains would come out of her favorite rug, your father's white shirt, your sister's party dress, the drapes, and various other odds and ends. You move around quite a lot during the ten seconds or so immediately following your first cut.

Sharpening the Knife—Acting on the folk wisdom of the day that it was the dull knife that cut fingers, you would get out the whetstone and hone your knife's blades, one big and one little, down to about one-half their former dimensions. Now you had what was known as a *sharp* knife. You would take the knife in to show your mother and father, and tell them, "Look, my knife's sharp as a razor!" Your father would smile and go back to reading his paper, and your mother would make a show of turning pale. Later you would wonder if maybe you had overplayed your hand in comparing the knife's sharpness to that of a razor.

Losing the Knife—The disappearance of your knife had a certain eerie quality to it. You would remember having placed the knife carefully on top of your dresser when you turned in for the night. The next morning it would be gone.

"I can't find my knife," you'd tell your father.

"What?" he'd yell. "You just got it! That knife set me back a whole dollar! How could you be so careless as to lose it already?" He would continue to carry on in such a fashion for the better part of an hour, the authenticity of his ravings relieving him of any suspicion in the knife's disappearance.

"I can't find my knife," you'd tell your mother.

"Don't bother me now," she'd say. "I have to sort the wash."

Somehow the urgency of your mother's having to sort the wash and the disappearance of your knife seemed related, but you could never find any real proof of maternal culpability.

Having once owned a knife, you now discovered that the craving to whittle was almost overpowering. You couldn't look at a piece of cedar kindling without being overcome with the urge to reduce it to shavings with your own pocketknife. But there were only two options open to you for acquiring a new knife. The first consisted of finding a job and earning enough money to buy one, but there were few employment opportunities for eight-year-olds. Consequently, you resorted to the child's version of the credit card: begging.

Sooner or later, begging would produce a second knife. The second knife would bear an uncanny resemblance to the first knife. Your mother would explain that she found it in the attic. Reluctantly offering it to you, she would advise, "Now don't cut yourself!"

Whittling was the main application of the pocketknife. You would whittle chains out of a single block of wood, as your grandfather had done, although you never progressed beyond the first link, which uninformed observers often mistook for a notch cut in the end of a piece of kindling.

Willow flutes were turned out by the gross. Inexplicably, the flutes would stubbornly refuse to produce a single toot, but they were great for humming through. Sometimes you could cut off the end of the flute and come up with a passable peashooter, which, smartly aimed, could produce a high C note from one of your associates.

Of all the satisfactions to result from owning a knife,

perhaps the greatest was the one of lending it to somebody, preferably a grownup, to perform some cutting chore. Sometimes you'd wait a year or two for such an opportunity. Then it would happen. You and a couple of your sidekicks would be standing about watching an adult perform some task, anything from undoing a sack of grain to overhauling an engine. No doubt the adult would have expressed some displeasure about the presence of his young audience, largely because it limited the use of colorful expressions in the release of frustration. You and the guys would be a bit nervous, but not enough to reduce your curiosity about the task being performed, or the hope you would get to hear a colorful expression. Then the adult would straighten up and dig into his pants pockets. Not finding what he sought, he would fix his attention on the spectators and speak the long-awaited words:

"Anybody got a knife on 'im?"

Ah, how delicious was the sound of that request! Even better was if the adult looked directly at you and asked, "Gotcher knife on ya?" *Your* knife. This indicated that the adult thought you the sort of mature and self-reliant and reliable person who would obviously carry a pocketknife.

If it happened that the other kids in the audience didn't have knives, had never owned knives, and even if they were only six or seven years old, they would still dig into their pockets and feel around among the contents in order to give the impression that they *usually*, almost *always*, had a knife on 'em but through some miserable stroke of fate had managed to leave it at home.

Your response to the question of whether you had a knife on you had been thought through months and possibly years in advance. If you were fortunate enough to be chewing on a toothpick, you would reach up slowly, deliberately, and remove the toothpick, then flick it back over your shoulder, possibly creating the impression in the adult that you couldn't chew a toothpick and reach for a knife at the same time, but no matter. There was a right way to do a thing and a wrong way, and this was the right way. Next you bent sideways from the hips, furrowed your brow slightly, and dug your hand into the pocket of your jeans, your fingers expertly sorting through such items as throwing rocks, a dried frog, a steel marble, your reserve wad of bubble gum, and the like, until they closed around the knife, *your* knife, the one that had been requested by an adult. You withdrew your knife with slow deliberation and expertly opened it, always selecting the big blade, of course. Then you handed it to the adult, who probably would have preferred to open the knife himself. And finally, at long last, you got to say it, not smugly or disrespectfully, of course, but matter-of-factly, *maturely*, and possibly with just the slightest touch of pride:

"Careful you don't cut yourself—that blade is razor sharp."

Nincompoopery
and Other
Group Terms

My dictionary informs me that the proper term for a group of larks is an *exaltation*. An exaltation of larks! That's wonderful! And it's so descriptively accurate.

You outdoorsmen probably think you're pretty smart and know all the terms for groups of creatures. We'll see about that right now.

Let's start with an easy one, a group of grouse. "Covey" you say, clapping your hands gleefully. But *covey* means a "family" of grouse. Suppose you have several families of grouse living together, what do you call that? If they're like the families I know, it would be a "mess." Actually, a group of grouse larger than a covey is a *pack*. In the interest of linguistic purity it is important to know the difference between a covey and a pack of grouse. To do this you must learn to distinguish between members of the immediate family and distant relations who have moved in for a bit of freeloading. This is not so difficult as you might think. The freeloaders are the grouse that get up at noon, go around unshaven, and keep asking, "What's for supper?"

Here's something a little tougher. What is the proper term for a group of ferrets? Don't just sit there scratching your head—guess. Okay, it's a *business* of ferrets. What business are the ferrets in? I don't know for sure, but it's probably loan-sharking.

The next term is a cinch—a group of geese. *Flock* is correct, but only if the geese are standing around killing time. If the group of geese is flying, it becomes a *skein*. If the geese are on the water, they're a *gaggle*. Subtract fifty points from your score if to any of the above you answered "a bunch of gooses."

One of my favorites among the terms for groups of creatures is a *crash* of rhinoceros. I can imagine an African guide saying to his client, "Shoot, dammit, shoot! Here comes the whole bloody crash of rhinoceros!"

You toad hunters out there probably don't even know that a group of toads is called a *knot*. Personally, I think I'd just as soon come across a crash of rhinoceros as a knot of toad.

Some of my other favorite group terms are

- A *convocation* of eagles. (Not to be confused with a convention of Eagles, who are the ones wearing hats.)
- A *charm* of hummingbirds.
- A *skulk* of foxes.
- A *chattering* of starlings.
- A *mustering* of storks.
- An *unkindness* of ravens.

- A *siege* of herons.
- A *leap* of leopards.
- A *murder* of crows.
- A *screaming meemie* of snakes. (I just tossed that in.)

To finish off this quiz and give you a chance to redeem yourself, here are two easy ones—a group of elk and a group of bears. The answers are a *gang* of elk and a *sloth* of bears. Surely you and your fellow outdoorsmen say things like, "All at once I found myself right in the middle of this gang of elk," or maybe, "Look, Fred! Here comes a sloth of bears! Run!"

I myself use all of the above terms, although it has been some time since I've come upon a leap of leopards. Actually, when it comes to group terms, I prefer "a whole mess of," which is easy to remember in tense situations, such as when a sloth of bears is heading your way.

Sadly, there are no group names for outdoorsmen, who deserve their own group terms just as much as do other wild creatures. In the interest of lexicography, I have invented my own group terms.

Let's begin with Cub Scouts. As with geese, the group terms vary according to what the Cubs are doing. If they are meeting at someone else's house, for example, they are referred to as a *den*. If they are meeting at your house, they are a *din* of Cub Scouts, a very important distinction, believe me! A group of den mothers, the adult leaders of Cubs, is a *frazzle*. Collectively, the husbands of den mothers are *the weekly poker game*.

There are different names for groups of fishermen in different situations. A group of fishermen driving out to begin a day of fishing is an *exuberance*. If the day turns out to be unsuccessful, the group is variously referred to as a *sulk* or a *grumble*. Fishermen surprised by a herd of mean cows (sometimes known as a *mayhem* of cows) become a *panic* of anglers or sometimes a *skein* of anglers. A group of ice fishermen is a *chatter* or a *chill*, although the term *loony* is often used, particularly by wives of ice fishermen.

As a group, spouses of fishermen off on a three-day lark, or even an exaltation of larks, are variously a *crash* of wives, a *leap* of wives, and sometimes a *murder* of wives. Often a single wife will appear to be a whole group under these circumstances and it is all right to use the appropriate group term, if you get the chance and think it will do you any good.

Strangely, there are few interesting group names for hunters. For example, a group of lost hunters is referred to as "a group of lost hunters," although wives will occasionally refer to such a group as a *nincompoopery*. A *boast* of hunters refers to any group of hunters larger than one. A *tedium* is any group of hunters who get started talking about their first deer, first elk, or any of their other firsts, of which there are whole exaltations.

As a child, I once joined a *berserk* of kid campers heading for home after a mountain lion screamed near our camp. It might have been a whole *pride* of mountain lions, for all I know, but even one was excessive.

A *whiff* of skunk trappers is one of my favorite group terms, as is a *cramp* of camp cooks.

But what's that? Did I just hear a lark beckoning me? Gee, it may even be several larks, a whole exaltation of them. It's been a long time since I've gone off on an exaltation. If there's not a leap of wife outside my door, I might go investigate.

Bad Company

Back when I was a kid, my mother constantly warned me about falling in with bad company. Then one day it occurred to her that I was probably the bad company, and she had to warn the other kids about falling in with me.

Personally, I've always preferred bad company to good. Bad company is so much more interesting. Outdoorsmen, and outdoorswomen too, for that matter, are the best of bad company. They have all these wild and terrible enthusiasms that inevitably lead to catastrophe. I don't much care for arriving at the catastrophe, but getting there can be a lot of fun.

Not everyone is cut out for bad company, however, and it is always sad to see such a person, a man or woman of sensibilities, fall in with the wrong crowd, which nine times out of nine consists of hunters and anglers. What usually happens is that the person of sensibilities becomes caught

up in the wave of enthusiasm generated by bad company
and gets swept along toward a catastrophe he doesn't expect
and isn't mentally or emotionally prepared for. Some people
just don't have the nerves or stomach for catastrophe.

I recall the time a nice young fellow by the name of
Farley overheard Retch Sweeney and me planning a hunting
trip and asked if he could come along. We said sure. Fortunately, it turned out to be an uneventful trip. I don't know
what would have happened if the outing had been typical,
because it soon became evident that poor Farley wouldn't
have been up to a full-scale catastrophe.

True, there was one small incident, but it's scarcely worth
mentioning. Retch slipped on some ice and grabbed Farley
by the arm, so that they both went down together. That's
about it. The fall couldn't have been more than ten feet.
Besides, the thin ice on the creek cushioned their fall and
prevented serious injury. Both Retch and I thought it was
hilarious, all that flailing of arms and legs as they went through
the ice, with Retch cussing a turquoise-blue streak and Farley
screaming.

I built a roaring fire so we could dry out their clothes,
and even let Farley wear my down jacket. He looked so
pitiful standing there naked and hunched over the fire, with
snowflakes falling on his bare skin. To cheer him up, I explained that the fire would probably attract the attention of
a search plane. After a hunting party has been lost in a
blizzard for four days, I told him, the National Guard usually
sends out a search plane. Then Retch and I tried to get him
to join in the joking and singing and other festivities, but
he would have none of it, choosing instead to stand around
looking morose, with his teeth chattering and his skinny blue
legs sticking out from under my jacket.

Later we invited Farley on another hunting trip, but he declined, rather brusquely I thought.

"Do you think it was something I done?" Retch said.

"No," I said. "I thought you treated him rather well, just as if he were one of the guys."

"Maybe he didn't like the coffee we had to make with water from mud puddles," Retch said. "He never caught on to the knack of straining out the pebbles with his teeth."

"That could have been it," I said. "Mostly, though, I think it was because he had too many sensibilities."

"Yeah, you're probably right. I had a sensibility once, and it was nothing but trouble."

The case of Farley serves to illustrate what happens when a person of sensibilities falls in with bad company but through rare good fortune avoids catastrophe. But suppose such a person doesn't avoid the standard catastrophe; what is the effect on him? Do his sensibilities survive? Does *he* survive? Is the money spent on therapy wasted? The following report answers these questions.

One day when I was about twelve, Rancid Crabtree and I discovered a bee tree high up on the mountain behind his place. An ancient logging road, grown over with brush and small trees, ran past the tall, silvery snag, which seemed fairly alive with thousands of bees busily and mindlessly storing more honey on top of the tons they had already no doubt collected over the years of undisturbed diligence.

"Hot dang!" Rancid said. "We got ourselves a honey tree!"

"So?" I said. "What good does it do us? We can't get the honey out of it without getting stung to death."

"Thet jist goes to show how little you knows about honey trees," Rancid said. "Shoot, thar ain't nothin' easier. The fust thang you does is to make a torch out of some rags, one thet'll put up a big cloud of smoke. Then you gits some gloves and heavy clothes the bees cain't sting through, and a hood of cheesecloth to protect the face. Then all that's left is to git the tree chopped down and the honey scooped up."

"It doesn't sound so easy to me."

"Waal, thet's because Ah ain't told you the best part yet. Once you git all the gloves and heavy clothes and the cheesecloth hood, you talks some dumb feller into puttin' 'em on and choppin' down the tree fer ya. Ha!"

"Not me!"

"No, not you. Even you ain't thet dumb! Ah was thankin' of Murph."

It was nearly dark before we tracked down Murph. He was lying on the floor in Fat Edna's tavern, with Fat Edna sitting on his chest.

"You take that back, you little shrimp," Fat Edna was saying.

"How you doin', Murph?" Rancid said.

"About the usual," Murph said. "How you?"

"Ah's fine. If you got a minute, Ah'd like to ask a favor of you."

Fat Edna grabbed Murph by the hair and thumped his head up and down on the floor. "Can't you see Murph's busy?"

Rancid hoisted Fat Edna off Murph. "You can finish this later. Ah needs to see if Murph knows anythang 'bout gittin' honey out of a bee tree without gittin' stung too bad."

There was plenty of bad company in the tavern that night, and upon hearing the mention of the bee tree, every last pitiful soul there rushed forward to offer a theory on how to get the honey away from the bees without getting stung. In no time at all, a great wave of enthusiasm began to build, a wave I later learned from association with bad company inevitably crashes down on the rocks of catastrophe.

Half the regulars of the tavern and Fat Edna herself soon piled out of the tavern and into cars and trucks to go help Rancid and me chop down the honey tree. Rancid drove Murph's truck, since he knew the way to the tree. Fat Edna squeezed into the cab with him, and Murph, Pinto Jack, and I, and several of the tavern's regulars jumped onto the truck bed. As we roared out of town, I noticed a stranger in the group. He was tall, thin, bald, and wearing a white suit that shimmered in the light of the moon.

"Hi," he said to me. "My name's Howard. This is so exciting, isn't it? My goodness, I just stopped by the tavern for a little nightcap before going to my hotel room, and now I'm involved in an adventure. What's your name, son?"

I told him. There was something that made me feel uneasy about Howard. He didn't seem to fit in with this crowd, which was very bad company indeed.

One of the regulars tilted up the communal jug of wine, took a swig, and then passed it to me. "Here, kid, give your frien' a drink." Although I never drank from a communal jug, or at all for that matter, I had studied the technique with care. I handed the jug to Howard. "You'd better take a drink," I said. Getting my drift, Howard studied the loathsome flotsam on the surface of the wine. Obviously none too pleased with the results of his study, he nevertheless shut his eyes and manfully took a tiny swig. The regulars and I almost gagged. Howard didn't realize that you are supposed to tilt the jug way back, so that the surface of the wine rises above the mouth and the drinker can sip from the clear wine beneath the flotsam. When you associate with bad company, bits of knowledge like that can be beneficial, both socially and hygienically. Ignorant though he might be of the finer points of etiquette, Howard had won our respect. The man had grit.

When we started lumbering up the overgrown mountain road, we lost most of the caravan of vehicles that had followed us from the tavern. The others soon gave up their pursuit and turned back when the road proved too treacherous. Our group of honey-seekers bounced and rattled about on the bed of the truck, seeking handholds where we could. One by one the regulars vibrated off the end of the truck, presumably to pick themselves up and stagger off down the mountain. By the time we reached the bee tree, the only survivors were Murph, Pinto Jack, Howard, and me, and of course Rancid and Fat Edna in the cab of the truck—still more than enough of us, however, to work up a major catastrophe.

"There's the bee tree!" I shouted, pointing to the silvery snag. The level of enthusiasm was instantly restored and everyone leaped from the truck shouting orders and advice, for that is the favorite activity of bad company.

"Fire up the torch," yelled Pinto Jack.

"Make the cheesecloth hood," shouted Rancid.

"Gimme my ax," cried Murph.

"My goodness," said Howard. "This is so exciting it gives me goosebumps."

The first order of business was a lengthy argument over how to chop down the tree.

"Notch her on the back," yelled Pinto Jack. "That will drop her alongside the road."

"And on top of my truck," shouted Murph. "No sir, she's got to drop downhill."

Without anything being settled, Murph, Pinto Jack, and

Rancid, all of them still shouting and arguing and calling each other names, went off toward the tree, carrying the ax, the heavy clothes, a lantern, and the smoky torch. Presently the ruckus died down, only to be replaced by ominous, hollow sounds of chopping. It occurred to me that Rancid, caught up in the wave of enthusiasm, had forgotten his own maxim of letting someone else do the dangerous work.

Fat Edna's cigarette glowed in the dark as she, Howard, and I stood listening to the attack on the bee tree.

"I sure hope nobody gets killed this time," Fat Edna said.

"How's that?" Howard asked. "Pardon?"

"Or maimed," Fat Edna added, looking at me. "You remember poor old Wally Jackson the time we tried to rope the bear that got into Murph's hog pen?"

"Yeah," I said. "Lefty Jackson."

"Lefty?" the man in the white suit said.

"And poor Harry Logan at the chainsaw races?"

"Yeah, Stumpy Logan."

"Stumpy?" the man in the white suit said. "Maybe we should . . ."

Suddenly the chopping ceased. "Ow!" somebody yelped, off in the darkness. And then somebody else shouted, "More smoke! More smoke! Ow! Ow!"

"I thought something like this might happen," Fat Edna said.

Rancid, Pinto Jack, and Murph rushed past us in a tight little cluster, slapping and howling. Then we too were caught up in a roaring tornado of angry bees.

"Ever'body into the truck cab!" yelled Rancid.

I was the last through the door, scrambling in on top of Fat Edna. Rancid fired up the truck, cut a U-turn, and we roared off down the mountain, dispatching bees as best we could in tight quarters. A catastrophe was in full progress.

"We missin' anybody?" Rancid asked. "Ow! Gol-durn bee! Whar's Murph? Ah don't see Murph!"

A muffled sound came from under Fat Edna. "I'm still here, but I'm going fast!"

"The man in the white suit!" I said. "He's not here!"

"Good gosh almighty," Rancid said. "The pore devil will git hisself stung to death!"

"I knew something like this would happen," Fat Edna said. "I just knew it!"

"Aaaaa," said Murph.

"What's that ahead?" said Pinto Jack.

The beam of the truck's single headlight illuminated a tall white figure sprinting down the road. Howard! I rolled down the window and yelled at him to jump on the running board. He jumped, hooking one arm over the door. Crouching on the running board, he screwed his face into a terrible expression as we roared into the first turn. Years later the image of his face at that moment would wake me in a cold sweat from my worst nightmares.

"Ever'body hold on, Ah got to hit the brakes fer the next tarn," Rancid said. "We'll never make it at this speed!"

The muffled voice of Murph came from under Fat Edna. "What brakes? This truck ain't got no brakes."

We hurtled around the curve, bounding over rocks and brush and small trees, Rancid wrestling the steering wheel as though it were a crazed beast. Then we shot over the brink of the last and steepest grade and plummeted toward the bottom of the mountain.

"We got her made now," Rancid said. "Leastwise, iffen we don't hit too hard." Then he glanced at the stranger, whose face was knotted up in one of the worst grimaces I've ever had the misfortune to witness. "You done real good, feller," Rancid complimented him. "Ain't ever'body could survive a ride like thet, with nothin' more to stand on than a runnin' board."

"What runnin' board?" Murph croaked. "This truck ain't got no runnin' board on that side."

Nobody at Fat Edna's ever again saw the man in the white suit. If he did pass through town, he chose not to stop by the tavern for a nightcap. Rancid said he sort of liked the stranger, too, but that there was something odd about him. Although I didn't say so, I knew what it was. Howard just wasn't cut out for bad company.

The Case of
the Missed Deer

The sun spread out against the western sky like a drop of blood on a blotter. The frozen ground under my feet felt like frozen ground, which was strange, since frozen ground usually feels like peanut brittle. I felt like a cigarette. If you don't know what a cigarette feels like, you probably don't read private-eye novels. Fictional private eyes often feel like cigarettes. Many of them even think like cigarettes. That is because private-eye novels are often writ ten by persons who write like cigarettes. It goes with the territory. I should know. I write private-eye novels.

That's why I was surprised when this outdoor editor called me up.

"McManus?"

"Yeah, that's me," I said, cradling the phone with my shoulder while I ground out a cigarette in the palm of my hand.

"What's wrong?" the editor asked. "Why the screech?"

"Nothing," I said.

"Why I'm calling," the editor continued, "is I want to hire you to write a hunting article."

"I get fifty dollars a day plus expenses," I said.

The editor laughed. "I heard you did humor, but I had no idea you were that funny! See if you can work some great jokes like that into the article." He hung up, chuckling.

Business had been slow lately. By "lately" I mean the last fifteen years. I decided to take the job.

The best part of writing a hunting article is the hunting. The writing comes later. That's when this business gets rough. I can't count the times I've stared into the cold muzzle of a blank sheet of paper. I won't even tell about the dangling participles that keep slipping up on you. And the commas! God, how I hate commas! Then there are the semicolons, the commas with the dots over them. I've never yet seen a semicolon that could be trusted. If you don't have guts enough to rub out a semicolon when you see one, you don't belong in this business.

As soon as the outdoor editor had hung up, I put on my hunting togs, slipped a gun into my shoulder holster, and headed for the door. My secretary, a tough blonde broad—or a tough broad blonde, to be more accurate—yelled at me.

"Hey, Nick, your gat is showing!"

I made a swift check of my person and immediately detected the cause of her alarm, at the same time allaying my own worst fear.

"That's a problem with these shoulder holsters," I said. "They're just too short for a rifle."

"What are you going after this time—deer?" Stella asked.

"I'm glad you asked that, sweetheart," I said. "I'm going after deer."

"Get lost!" she riposted.

That's how I came to be standing behind a tree on a mountainside, running a surveillance on a clearing directly ahead of me. The sun was no longer like a drop of blood on a blotter. It was more like a smear of orange marmalade on burnt toast. The frozen ground still felt like frozen ground, but I now felt like peanut brittle. It was cold.

Doc Watson accompanied me on the hunt. He is not a real doctor but a Ph.D. in economics. Despite this handicap, Doc has a tremendous sense of humor. Whenever people hear him referred to as "Doc," they assume he is a medical doctor and start asking for advice. Ol' Doc loves to string people along, sometimes telling them that the prime rate is too high and may cause their business to fall off. This almost always scares the bejeebers out of them. As a joke, he once performed an appendectomy. It was hilarious.

"Something's wrong here, Doc," I said. "I was supposed to meet a deer in this clearing and it hasn't shown up."

"Three deer have already walked across the clearing," Doc said.

"How come I didn't see them?"

"Because you're standing behind a tree."

That's the kind of mind Doc has—sharp! He can analyze a complex situation instantly. Moving only six inches to one side, I discovered that the trunk of the tree no longer blocked my vision.

"Well, I'll be danged," I said. "The solution was so obvious. Why didn't I see it?"

"Possibly it's because you had your mind on other matters," Doc analyzed. "On the other hand, it's probably because you're dumb."

On the far side of the clearing, the brush parted and a nice buck stepped out. He was a big old fellow, and I could tell he had been around and knew the score, which was Deer—15, Me—0. That is why he sauntered casually along, broadside to me and no more than fifty yards away. He was close enough that I could see the smirk on his face. Such insolence in a deer is unforgivable, and I decided to settle his venison right then and there.

In a smooth, swift motion, I brought the rifle to firing position, neatly dislocating my left shoulder. In my haste, I'd forgotten to remove the rifle from its holster. Shrugging off the pain, I danced around yelling and cursing.

"Good thing I brought my bag with me," Doc said. "I may have to remove that shoulder if it becomes inflationary."

I gave Doc a hard look. He was standing there smugly eating a sandwich.

"Just for that, I'm going to waste that turkey," I snarled.

Doc looked startled. "Why don't you waste the pastrami instead? I'm eating the turkey."

With a sardonic laugh, I snatched the sandwich from his hands and ground it under my boot. Instantly I felt better.

"Let that be a lesson to you," I told Doc. "And if you don't shut up, I'm going to waste your fruit drink and pudding cup."

Doc has no stomach for violence, although his liver enjoys a Clint Eastwood film from time to time. He walked off a ways to pout.

Surprisingly, the deer was still standing in the clearing watching us, his smirk now transformed into a broad grin. I settled the crosshairs of the scope just behind his front shoulder and squeezed the trigger. It was an easy shot. So easy, in fact, that there was no way I could miss. Afterwards, I even felt a little ashamed. The least I could have done was to give the buck a sporting chance. That would have explained the miss. But to miss him while he was just standing there grinning at me! It was humiliating.

"What's the score now?" Doc asked.

"Deer—16, Me—0," I said.

"And you have to write a hunting article about this," Doc said. "How are you going to do that?"

"With great difficulty," I said. "But I've got to do it."

Driving back to town, I told Doc about the kinds of atrocities editors had committed on writers who didn't get articles in on time. He shuddered.

"Maybe you could just make up something," Doc said. "That's what we economists do. Heck, just say that you got the deer. Who's to know?"

"I can't do that," I said. "But I think I've figured a way out of this mess. I'll just tell the truth."

"It's easy to see you're no economist," Doc said. "What's your angle?"

"Well," I replied, "I thought I'd start off with 'The sun spread out against the western sky like a drop of blood on a blotter.' "

Character Flaws

As an outdoorsman, you frequently run the risk of finding yourself locked into a week-long stay at a remote hunting camp with a person you barely know. By the end of the week, you know the person very well indeed, and may fervently wish you didn't. This problem can be avoided by putting any new acquaintance through a series of psychological tests to determine his mental and emotional shortcomings, just in case you are ever forced to spend a week with him at a remote hunting camp.

Before committing yourself to a hunt with any new acquaintance, you should first take him on an overnight camping trip, one of the very best of all psychological tests. Then note the following indicators to his qualities as a hunting-camp companion.

Grub can be an excellent indicator of flawed character. For example, if the fellow cooks up a supper consisting of fried wieners, fried cabbage, fried potatoes, fried beans, fried bread, and fried custard, he is obviously all right. Give him five bonus points if, as a final course to the meal, he serves individual bowls of Tums with whipped topping.

On the other hand, if the chap attempts to feed you something like boiled beets, he should be regarded with suspicion. Clinical psychologists universally interpret the act of serving boiled beets to armed men as evidence of a massive psychological disorder. The man obviously has no inkling what the mere sight of boiled beets can do to the morale of exhausted hunters who have spent the day tramping up and down mountains in a freezing rain. Under such circumstances, a small serving of boiled beet cubes once caused Retch Sweeney to sob uncontrollably for over an hour. The perpetrator of the crime was quite upset by the incident, as he probably would have been even if Retch hadn't been twisting his arm.

Green hash provides another good test for character flaws. Cook up your own special recipe and serve it to the subject. (Since you are on a camping trip lasting only a couple of days, you may have to use green food coloring, rather than allowing the green to develop naturally, as it does in the typical hunting camp.) Note the reaction of the subject to the green hash. Does he politely gobble it down without complaint? Does he jump back and hit at it with a stick? Such nuances of behavior can tell you much about the individual's character. Obviously, no rational person will eat green hash, nor will experienced hunters. Keep in mind that if you decide to conduct the test with naturally green hash, any subject who eats it won't be available for the hunting trip anyway, thus saving you the embarrassment of telling him he can't go. A get-well card is optional.

The subject's response to discomfort should be carefully

noted during the test camping trip. Does he howl and yelp over every dozen mosquito bites, moan all through the night because his sleeping bag is wet, complain bitterly because the campfire smoke gets in his eyes, and so on? Or does he cheerfully accept these discomforts as a matter of course? As the true outdoorsman knows, anyone who cheerfully accepts the discomforts of camp as a matter of course is absolutely unbearable and should be rejected without question.

Check to see if the individual has a sense of humor. In the middle of the night, seal him in his sleeping bag by placing a few wraps of duct tape over the bag's zipper. Then slosh him with a pail of cold water and yell, "Run for your life! The dam broke!" When you present him with the prize for "fastest hopping in a sleeping bag," does he smile? If so, it is probably safe to let him out of the sleeping bag. Whether you wish later to spend ten days in a wild and remote area with this individual is up to you.

The prospective hunting-camp companion should have a sense of modesty. Nothing is quite so embarrassing as having a member of the group running around stark naked. For this test, hide the subject's clothes in the typical manner associated with most hunting camps. Then note carefully whether he wraps himself in a towel before chasing you with a hatchet.

Does the subject willingly jump in and do his share of the camp chores? Such people generally turn out to be excruciating bores, as well as making all the other hunters in camp feel guilty.

Is the subject particularly keen on hunting? Check this out by questioning him thoroughly. I have on occasion been in hunting camps where one individual would insist upon going out hunting every day. As another hunter once commented, "What does Joe think we come all the way out to this hunting camp for, to hunt? The guy's weird. Now whose turn to deal?"

(Oddly, many nonhunters think the reason hunters go off to remote hunting camps is to hunt. Your wife, for example, may express surprise when you reply to her question of whether you had any luck, "Not bad. I won thirty bucks." Since the expression of her surprise will consist only of a very slight elevation of one eyebrow, you have to watch closely for it.)

Storytelling skill ranks as one of the most important qualities in a prospective hunting-camp companion. The test consists of asking the subject about one of his scars. Suppose he replies, "You mean this little scar on my thumb? I got that on a broken bottle when I reached into a grocery sack. Why do you ask?" Then, of course, he flunks. Any halfway decent storyteller should be able to get at least twenty minutes' worth of story out of any scar. Technique should also be studied. In response to the inquiry regarding the scar on his thumb, does the subject stare off into the distance as if reflecting on the miracle that the thumb is still attached to his hand? This indicates that he is making up a really good story about the scar, complete with gory details. Hunters like a story with lots of gory details, even though they are not going to believe a word of it. WARNING: Any hunter who can go for more than two hours on a single scar should be considered for rejection. He is too good and will demoralize his companions to the extent that even the fellow who had his leg half gnawed off by a panther will hesitate to mention it.

Is the subject overly cautious? Does he bring along an

extra set of clothes in case he falls in a river or something? A hunter possessing this absurd character flaw should be shown tolerance and invited along to the hunting camp. Making allowances for such a hunting companion is always desirable, although not to the extent that he varies from you by more than one size either way.

Does the subject enjoy a good practical joke? Or does he sleep with a cocked revolver in one hand and a machete in the other? Such a mannerism can take much of the fun out of practical-joking. Try a few mild practical jokes on the subject. By "mild" I mean stop short of building a fire in one of his boots, for example. Sewing the rear flap shut on the subject's longjohns should also be avoided. Should your hand slip, it is too difficult to explain to a relatively new acquaintance why you interrupted his sleep by poking him with a needle. Many promising new friendships have ended for lesser cause.

That completes the psychological examination. If the subject passes all these tests, he will make the perfect hunting-camp companion. On that basis alone, he must be rejected. Who wants to spend a week in a remote hunting camp with some guy who's perfect?

Mean Tents

I once shot three arrows through my cousin Buck's brand-new wall tent. This may not seem remarkable to you, but it was to Buck. I can still recall several of his remarks, in fact, even though at the time they were made, I was vaulting a high board fence as he tried to tear off one of my legs. It happened like this.

I was out in Buck's backyard, practicing with his bow and arrows, when he showed up carrying a large bundle of canvas on his shoulder. Buck was four years older than I, or about twenty. He had a job and could afford to buy all kinds of neat hunting and fishing stuff. I could use his stuff anytime I wanted, provided Buck wasn't around. His mother, my Aunt Sophie, who thought highly of me, was always eager to help the less fortunate, who in this case happened to be me. She would unlock the door to Buck's bedroom and even help me disarm some of the booby traps her ingenious son had set to maim or kill me, should I sneak in to use his stuff.

"What are you doing with my bow?" Buck snarled, even though it was perfectly obvious I was target-practicing.

Pretending not to hear, I said, "Gosh, Buck, what's that you got there?"

Instantly his mood flip-flopped. "A new wall tent!" he exclaimed. "I just bought it. Wait till you see this baby. I'm gonna take it up into the mountains next fall and set up a hunting camp like you wouldn't believe. I got this little wood-stove I'm gonna put in it for heat, and a little table and chairs, and a couple of cots . . ."

Having distracted him from uncharitable thoughts about my use of his bow, I helped him drag the tent across the backyard to a flat area about ten feet from the bale of hay I had been using as a target. We soon had the tent pitched, its canvas taut and gleaming in the sun. I had to admit it was a nice-looking tent. Buck thought it was beautiful. We stepped back to admire it.

While he was in such a good mood, I said, "Yeah, that's a terrific tent, Buck. Mind if I shoot a few more arrows?"

"What? Oh, yeah, go ahead. Now, you see that canvas? It's special canvas. That canvas is windproof and . . ."

I casually let fly with an arrow at the target. The arrow curved like a boomerang in flight and, with a tiny *phutt!*, zipped through the roof of the tent.

". . . waterproof." Buck's eyes widened. His jaw gaped slowly, as if held by a weak spring.

"It was an accident, Buck," I cried, snatching up another arrow. "Your arrow must have been crooked. See, I shot it just like this."

Phutt! The second arrow had zipped through the tent!

I could not believe this was happening. It was as if the

tent had a magnetic attraction for arrows. I glanced at Buck. He seemed okay, except for possible paralysis of his entire nervous system. His lips made little jerking motions, but otherwise he was immobile.

"I can explain, Buck. Some of these arrows are crooked. They curve when you shoot them. Now this arrow is straight. Watch, it'll hit the target. Those other two arrows were crooked. It's not my fault you have crooked arrows. Here goes."

Phutt!

It was the strangest occurrence I had ever encountered. Having considerable interest in science, I would have liked to study how not one, not two, but three arrows could be drawn ten feet off course and through the roof of a tent. By this time, however, Buck had come unthawed and un-wrapped, cutting short any hopes I might have had for dis-covering the attraction of tent canvas for arrows. I took my usual escape route over the back fence, sacrificing only half a pantleg to the clawing hands of my crazed cousin.

Thirty years later Buck would still be convinced that I had deliberately shot the arrows through the tent for no better reason than to aggravate him. But I was innocent. The guilty party was the tent itself, its motive nothing more than to cause me trouble. In fact, tents have always had it in for me.

Remember the old Interior-Frame Umbrella Tent? The one with the contraption called the "spider" that was sup-posed to hold everything together? We used one of those tents for fifteen years. Every camping family in America owned one. Few people know, however, that they were orig-inally developed by research psychologists as a stress test to determine the limits of sanity. Later, the U.S. Army got

ahold of the I-FUT, as the Interior-Frame Umbrella Tent
was known, and experimented with it as a means of training
recruits in hand-to-hand combat. When it was rejected by
the army as too demoralizing to the troops, tent manufac-
turers decided the I-FUT was perfect for campers. After
all, they reasoned, campers go out seeking hardship and
adventure. Pitching the I-FUT would provide the average
camper with about all the hardship and adventure he could
stand.

Even though we last used our I-FUT more than ten years
ago, before we moved up to the Exterior-Frame Tent, I can
still recall vividly the typical routine of pitching it:

I have just staked down the floor of the tent. The tent
came with tough plastic stakes, which greatly eased this task,
but of course all of the stakes have now been lost. I have
substituted crooked pieces of tree branch for the plastic
stakes, pounding them in with a flat rock. This results in my
having to perform the Crouch Hop, a primitive dance in
which the performer holds one hand between his thighs and
hops about chanting "Hai-yi-yi-yi!" and other chants, while
his wife holds her hands over the ears of the youngest child.

Now comes the dreaded part. I must crawl into the
shapeless mass of canvas to insert the interior frame. Pow-
dery remains of last year's insects come sprinkling down onto
my face. The tiny, stickery legs are the worst, particularly
when they go down the back of your shirt collar. I sneeze.
As a cause of sneezing, powdered bug is just as bad as pepper. Some people think it's a whole lot worse. Squeamish
people almost always abandon camping during this phase
of pitching the I-FUT.

Not all the bugs are dead. At least one daddy longlegs
will have survived the winter for the sole purpose of racing

up under your pantleg. When you are standing in the dark with a collapsed tent around your head, a daddy longlegs racing for your vitals feels as big as a Dungeness crab.

The part of the frame called the "spider" has four arms, each of which extends out to a corner of the roof tent. The upright poles, in theory at least, insert into the outer ends of the spider arms. A short, sharp-edged pipe protrudes downward from the center of the spider. The sharp end of this pipe is placed on top of your head to hold the spider in place while you attach the poles. This explains why all old-time tent campers have a series of little overlapping circles on the tops of their heads.

I am now standing in the tent with one spider charging up my leg and the other "spider" cutting doughnut holes in my scalp. Quickly I insert the first pole into the spider, but it won't stay in place by itself until another pole has taken the slack out of the tent. I balance on one leg and hold the pole up with the other.

"Quick," I yell to my little helpers outside. "Hand Daddy another pole." I immediately hear the sound of scurrying feet, followed by heated argument.

"I got it first! Leggo!"

"Aaaaaah," I say. "Just get Daddy the pole!"

"Daddy wants me to do it! Give it here!"

"Aaaaaahh!" I say. "Hur-reeee! Aaaah!"

"Gimme that pole!"

"Aaakkkk!" I say.

"I got it! Here I come, Daddy!"

I can hear little feet charging for the door of the tent. "Easy! Easy!" I yell, but too late. The pole comes through the flap of the tent like a spear thrust.

"Just think," my wife says later, "if we had just one more

kid, you could stand one in each corner of the tent to hold a pole while you hook up the spider."

"That possibility has just been rendered academic," I say. "So maybe we'll buy a camper."

I still have our old I-FUT out in the corner of the garage, and it's in surprisingly good shape. My wife says I should donate it to the Salvation Army so it can be passed on to a needy family. I point out to her that needy families already have enough problems without my inflicting an I-FUT on them. Besides, I like to keep the I-FUT around for old times' sake. Whenever I get depressed, I can go out and kick it hard several times. Immediately I feel better.

My very first tent was a tepee. I made it out of three crooked branches and a blanket when I was about six years old. It served me well for an hour or two, until I decided to take the chill out of the air by building a fire in it. Presently my father came wandering out of the house and saw me standing by my tepee, which was putting up little puffs of smoke. It is a traumatic experience, let me tell you, for a small child to see his father stomp out his tepee! To complicate matters, Dad never understood what it was he had stomped out. He thought I just liked to set fire to blankets.

Speaking of strained relations between father and son, I'm reminded of the time a couple of years later that Crazy Eddie Muldoon and I made a tent out of gunnysacks. We had found the sacks in the back of the Muldoon barn. Although they were moldy and half rotten and flecked with dried cow manure, Eddie said they would still make a good tent. We obtained a large pair of shears and a curved sacking needle from his father's toolbox, which Mr. Muldoon had thoughtfully left within our reach. By suppertime the tent was finished.

I tried to conceal my disappointment over the appearance of the finished product. To me it looked more like a large, shaggy cocoon than a tent. Crazy Eddie, however, was delighted with it, as he was with all his creations.

"We'll set it up in the backyard and sleep in it tonight," he announced.

"Okay," I said. Eddie and I had been trying to sleep out all night in his backyard for most of the summer, but our efforts had always been thwarted by the elements—torrential darkness being the most frequent. So far, our best time had been 9:30. But Eddie had recently discovered a secret weapon: his father's powerful, six-battery flashlight. Furthermore, his father was away on a trip and not expected back until late that night. We would simply leave the flash light on all night and return it to his father's shop in the morning before he was awake and hovering about, eyeing us with suspicion. Mr. Muldoon would never know the difference. It would teach him a good lesson, too, for guffawing and teasing us about our failures at sleeping out past 9:30, even though we gave him detailed reports on the large, weird creatures we had seen prowling the yard.

The disaster resulting from this innocent plan cannot be properly understood without knowing the exact sequence of events, which is as follows:

7:30 p.m.: Crazy Eddie and I haul a quilt, a blanket, and two pillows out to our tent and make our bed.

8:00 p.m.: We crawl under the quilt and lie there looking at the stars through the roof of our tent. We have routinely checked the laces on our tennis shoes for tightness. Kids we know have thrown a shoe coming out of the starting blocks on their way into the house on a dark night. The loss of traction on one side has caused them to waste precious seconds running in a circle.

9:00 p.m.: The condition known as "pitch dark" has been

achieved. Crazy Eddie flips on the powerful flashlight. The beam shoots out through our tent and illuminates the countryside for a hundred yards. It seems adequate. Eddie and I exchange smiles of confidence.

10:00 p.m.: Mrs. Muldoon turns off the house lights and goes to bed. Only the feeble porch light remains on. A sense of apprehension fills the gunnysack tent. The beam of the flashlight has weakened.

10:15 p.m.: Mr. Muldoon gets in his car and begins the long drive home. He turns on the radio to listen to country-western music.

11:00 p.m.: The power of the flashlight has diminished to that of a firefly. The porch light provides some illumination. A dark shadow passes over the tent. Eddie and I dig starting blocks with the heels of our tennis shoes through the floor of the tent.

11:05 p.m.: Mr. Muldoon flicks the radio dial to "The Creaking Door." Tonight's program is about a mummy that tracks down and takes revenge on an archaeologist for disturbing its tomb. Mr. Muldoon shudders at the dry, rustling sound of the mummy's loose wrappings as they drag across the floor. The mummy says, "Urrr-uh! Urrr-uh!" which may not be all that articulate, but is pretty good for a mummy.

11:25 p.m.: Mr. Muldoon pulls into his driveway. On the radio, the archaeologist is screaming, "No! No! Stay away from meeeee!" Then there's the sound of wrappings scraping across the floor. "Urrr-uh," says the mummy. "Urrr-uh!" Mr. Muldoon shuts off the radio, gets out of the car, and heads for the house. Then he goes back and shuts off the car lights. The wind rustles in the bushes. Mr. Muldoon rushes into the house and turns on the lights.

Eddie and I have heard Mr. Muldoon drive in. Our

flashlight is dead. Our tennis shoes are dug into the starting blocks, but now we must wait for Mr. Muldoon to go to bed. Otherwise he will tease us unmercifully. Outside, there is a strange rustling sound, coming closer and closer. It's a good thing we haven't heard the mummy program.

11:35 p.m.: Mr. Muldoon shuts off the kitchen light *and* the porch light. He has no reason to expect his son and me to be outside after 9:30. He goes into the bathroom to take a shower, still thinking about the mummy.

11:45 p.m.: The rustling around the tent has increased. Eddie is fumbling with the knots on the door, but can't untie them in the dark. In a few minutes, Mr. Muldoon will be in bed asleep.

11:46 p.m.: Eddie's dog, Oscar, returns from a date at a neighboring farm and slumps down exhausted on the porch. Oscar has no reason to expect Eddie and me to be outside after 9:30.

11:50 p.m.: Mr. Muldoon thinks he detects a sore throat coming on. He walks into the darkened kitchen, pours some salt into a glass of hot water, and begins to gargle. He is wearing only a towel, wrapped around his middle.

11:50:30 p.m.: Eddie groans. "I can't get these dang knots untied in the dark. Let's go inside. We can take the tent off in there." A shadow passes over the tent, accompanied by a rustling sound to our rear. We shove our feet through the burlap floor and, hugging the tent around us, hit the starting blocks.

11:50:31 p.m.: On the porch, Oscar opens his bleary eyes. A large, amorphous shape is charging him! Almost on top of him! Probably going to eat him! He tries to bark but has momentarily swallowed his tongue. "Urrr-uh!" he growls. "Urrr-uh!"

11:50:32 p.m.: Eddie and I crash through the door into

the kitchen. Instantly we hear a horrible sound. We don't know what it is, never before having heard a naked man surprised in mid-gargle by a gunnysack tent. Oscar follows us into the house, still trying to bark. "URRR-UH! URRR-UH!" Water splashes on the floor and there is the sound of naked feet frantically trying to get traction on slippery linoleum.

"Gargle, gurgle, choke!" cries Mr. Muldoon. "St-stay—*hack, gargle*—away—*choke*—from meeeeee!"

We didn't get the mess all sorted out and reconstructed until the next morning. Mr. Muldoon seemed quite embarrassed by the whole episode, and never again teased us for abandoning a backyard camp in the middle of the night. Later, though, he enjoyed recalling the episode of the gunnysack tent and having a good laugh over it. I was away at college by then, however, and never got to hear him.

Crick Ritual

Retch Sweeney is on the phone. "Want to go fish the crick tomorrow?"

"Oh, I suppose so," I say. "What time you want to leave?"

"Four sharp," he says. "You know the crick. The best fishin' is always at first light."

"Okay."

Note the casualness of the conversation, the hint of indifference. The tone conceals any hint of reverence for the proposed undertaking—to go fish the crick. But both Retch and I know that we speak of solemn and elaborate ritual. We are talking religious experience here, mysticism, transcendentalism even.

Yes, transcendentalism. What we hope to transcend is time—thirty, forty years of time, back to the days of ancient summers with the crick flowing through our fresh, untarnished lives.

Rituals must be performed with precision. One flaw, one

misstep, one missed cue, and the spell is broken. I must take care tomorrow to do everything exactly right. Otherwise, my one day of fishing the crick this year will be ruined, and I will be left with insufficient mental, emotional, and spiritual resources to sustain me for the next twelve months.

"Where's my black tenner shoes?" I ask my wife.

"You mean those wading shoes you blew eighty dollars on? They're in your closet."

"Not those. The black tenner shoes with the little rubber ankle patches that are starting to peel off. The ones that are worn through on the sides."

"Oh, no! Don't tell me it's time for you and Retch to fish the creek again!"

"Crick," I correct her. "The proper technical term for this sort of stream is 'crick.' A creek is something entirely different."

"Well, your tenner shoes, as you call them, are out in a corner of the garage where you left them a year ago."

"Good," I say. "You haven't seen my fish pole, have you?"

"What do you mean? You have twenty or thirty fishing rods on the wall of your office."

"I know where the rods are. What I'm looking for is the fish pole. It's steel and has three sections that telescope into each other, kind of green and rusty. It's got the old bait-casting reel on it, the one that makes the horrible sound because of all the sand in the gears."

"Oh, that one. It's out in the garage by your tenner shoes."

Early the next morning I head over to Retch's. I have brewed myself a large vacuum bottle of strong coffee and constructed a delicious lunch: thick sandwiches of fresh homemade bread piled high with roast beef, cheese, and onion; a banana; an orange; two candy bars; and a slab of apple pie. It makes my mouth water to think of the lunch, nestled there next to my bottle of rich black coffee. There? Too late I remember the coffee is still on the kitchen table with my lunch next to it. Drat! Damn all kitchen tables, those incorrigible thieves of fishermen's lunches!

It's nearly six when I arrive at Sweeney's house, two hours late. He will be steamed. I ring the doorbell. Five minutes later Retch opens the door. He is still in his pajamas.

"Wha'?" he says. "What are you doin' here in the middle of the night?"

"It's six o'clock," I snap. "Remember? We're going to go fish the crick today? I've been waiting out in the yard two hours for you to wake up!"

"Good gosh, the crick! That's right! Look, I'm sorry. Don't be mad."

"Oh, all right. It's just that I have such high regard for punctuality."

Retch leaves and returns a few minutes later. He is wearing his rotten old tenner shoes and carrying his fish pole. There is a dried worm on the hook that dangles beneath a quarter pound of split-shot sinkers.

"What kind of leader you got on?" I ask.

"Twenty-pound," he says. "The usual."

"Good," I say. "We don't want any fish bustin' off. Now where are the worms?"

"Worms?" Retch says. "You was supposed to dig the worms."

"Oh, no! I dug them last year, remember?"

"Yeah, I got an exact recollection. I dug 'em. And the year before that, too. Well, c'mon, let's go dig some out behind the woodshed. Grab the shovel. You can dig and I'll pick up the worms."

"Why don't you dig and let me pick up the worms?"

" 'Cause it's my shovel, that's why."

We go out behind the woodshed, I spade up half an acre of ground, and we find only three scrawny worms. The next day Retch will plant his garden in the area I spaded up, but he fails to mention his plan to me now.

"Hey, I know where we can find some worms," he says. "Over in my compost pile."

In five minutes we fill the can half full of worms from his compost pile. Odd that he didn't think of the compost pile first. Mysteries like this tend to nag at one's mind.

I suggest that we divide the worms between two cans, but Retch says no, we will be fishing together so we can both use the same can. Besides, he says, he has only one good worm can.

It is ten o'clock when we arrive at the crick and start fishing. As Retch says, ten o'clock is the best time to start fishing the crick, because the fish were expecting us for the early-morning feed and will now be caught off guard. I agree.

The crick, still fed by melting snows in the mountains, is icy cold. We rule out trying to wade it, which means that we must hurl our lines over the wall of brush bordering the crick on our side and listen for the splash of the sinkers hitting the water. No splash means the hook snagged on a branch above the water, where it's unlikely to attract fish. We make several casts without hearing a splash. We then decide to cross to the far bank, which has less brush. We will cross the crick on two strands of barbwire, the remains of an old fence suspended above the water. The trick to crossing a stream on such a fence is to walk on the bottom wire and hold on to the top wire for balance.

Retch bounces on the fence over the middle of the crick.

He begins to lean forward, pushing the top wire ahead of him with his hands, the bottom wire out behind with his feet. "Hanhh hannhh hanh!" he says, but I am uncertain as to what this means. He reverses his posture and is now leaning backward over the crick. "Hannnnhhh!" he repeats, but with no more clarity of meaning. He gives the top wire a vicious pull, and faster than the eye can follow, flips forward. His body is now parallel to the crick, facedown, about a yard above the water, straining between the two screeching strands of wire. "Gah gah gah!" he says. I cannot help but be amused by this marvelous acrobatic performance, but enough is enough.

"Stop fooling around," I say. "You're going to drop the worm can."

My admonishment comes too late. His belly sags toward the water, even though he makes a valiant effort to suck it back up. He now makes a sound similar to that of a dog tugging on a rag—ERRRrrrrERRR! Then there is a whir and a yelp, and Retch plops into the crick.

I knew he would mess around until something like this happened! "Don't drop the worm can!" I yell. "Don't drop the worms!"

Ignoring my admonition, he splashes out of the crick on the far side, his mouth spewing out a stream half crick and half profanity. This is a bad omen.

I walk around a bend in the crick and find a cottonwood log that a considerate family of beavers had the decency to chew down so that it fell from one bank across to the other. Many people do not like beavers, but . . . Halfway across the log, I notice that the spatula-tailed vandals have maliciously chewed a section of the far end down to the dimensions of a toothpick! I try to retreat. Too late.

"Pretty fast moves there," Retch says. "The first five steps across the water you hardly sunk a bit. But that sixth step was a doozie."

"Very funny," I say, wringing out my hat while waiting for Retch to stop cackling. "Since we're wet and freezing anyway, we may as well just wade down the crick. I'm glad to see you didn't lose the worms. Give me a handful of them. I don't want to chase after you every time I need a worm."

"Whatcha gonna put 'em in?"

"Why, my pants pocket, of course. They might ice up a bit in there, but I don't think it will hurt them, except they might not be able to have any more children."

About noon, the fish start biting. Two of them, a small one and a big one. We put them on a forked stick and divide the rest of the day between fishing and trying to find the last place we laid the forked stick. Retch deliberates whether he should eat the big fish or have it mounted. I mention it will cost him ten dollars an inch to get it mounted.

"In that case, I better eat it," he says. "I don't have an extra eighty dollars."

We pass up the best fishing hole on the crick. I am tempted to try for a quick cast on my way past the hole, but I might break my stride. That's what fast, mean cows watch for, a break in the fisherman's stride, and then they've got him.

"Shall we—*pant*—try to—*pant*—vault the fence or—*pant*—roll under it?" Retch says.

I glance back. The nearest cow is fifteen inches behind us and gaining. "Vault."

We vault and land safely on the other side of the fence. Not bad for a couple of pudgy, fifty-year-old men. The few little pieces of us left on barbwire are relatively unimportant.

We slip down to the Old Packard hole. It is called the Old Packard hole because years ago someone dumped an old Packard into the crick there. My cousin Buck once drifted a worm through the broken windshield of the Packard and caught a big fat brookie out of the back seat. It is now late in the day. I think just possibly Buck's brookie's great-great-great-great-great-great-grandchild might have taken up residence there. So for my final effort of the day I drift a worm through the windshield of the old Buick. The worm drifts down into the dark water of the back seat. I twitch the line ever so gently. I wait. Perhaps there is no big fat brookie there, I think. Then, like a flash of lightning, it happens: I am struck by the revelation that I am never going to catch a fish out of the Old Packard hole. Retch and I give up and head for home.

Driving back to town, wet, cold, exhausted, bruised, cut, and punctured, with only two measly fish between us, we stare silently ahead.

"I kind of expected it would turn out like this, the way the day started," Retch says. "You forgot your lunch, I forgot to set my alarm clock, we had to dig up half the countryside to find any worms, we both fell in the crick right away and then got chased by cows, all for two little fish."

"Yeah," I say. "It was perfect, wasn't it?"

"Yep," Retch says, grinning. "Just like when we was kids. Funny, ain't it, how after all these years we can remember how to do everything just right."

"That's what a ritual is," I say. "Doing it all just right."

Now my wife is shrieking down in the laundry room. After all these years, you would think she would know better than to reach into a fisherman's pants pockets, especially after he has just returned from performing a crick ritual.

Hunting Camp
Etiquette

Once again it is time for my question-and-answer column in which I dispense bits of wisdom, helpful hints, and an occasional downright dangerous piece of advice. The topic for today is "Hunting Camp Etiquette."

Dear PFM:

I am just getting started in the sport of hunting. Last fall I happened to ask the camp cook what was in the stew. Everyone seemed shocked by my question. The cook went into his tent and pouted for the rest of the evening. What did I say wrong?

Puzzled in Detroit

Dear Puz:

The one question you never ask a camp cook is "What's in the stew?" You can be quite certain the cook does not wish to reveal the contents of any of his dishes, even if he knows what they are.

The other hunters present want even less to hear the concoction described in any detail. Simply eat your stew like a man and don't ask questions. Afterwards, however, you should try to monitor your vital functions for at least two hours.

Another problem with asking the cook about his stew is that it may not be stew. It may be hash or scrambled eggs or pancakes, which could explain why the cook went to his tent to pout. Can you blame him?

Dear PFM:

I have trouble getting to sleep the first night in camp. The other fellows in my tent seem to drop right off the minute they hit the sack. Then they start to snore, which makes it even more difficult for me to get to sleep. Is there any polite way of inducing them to stay awake until I fall asleep?

Nodding-off in Birmingham

Dear Nod:

Yes, there are two proven methods for doing this. If you have had stew for supper, a mere suggestion planted in the minds of the other hunters can be quite effective in keeping them awake for hours. As soon as everyone is in his sleeping bag, simply shout out, "I can't feel my legs! I can't feel my legs!" This is a wonderful way of gaining the attention of the other hunters. They all leap up and rush off to the nearest poison center. Try to get some sleep before they return.

Another ploy is to wait until the other guys are nearly asleep and then say, "What the devil was that? Did you guys hear that weird sound?" The only thing that remains to do then is to plump up whatever it is you are using for a pillow and get some shuteye. The other guys will lie awake for hours, listening.

Dear PFM:

We had a fellow in camp this year who kept asking things like, "Tell me again, which side of the trees does the moss grow on?" Should a person like this be allowed to wander away from camp by himself?

Wondering in Seattle

Dear Won:

Only if he is your guide. I once had a guide who constantly argued with his compass. "That can't be north," he would say. "This stupid compass shows north in the southeast! Stupid instrument! Well, forget that! This way, guys. The road has to be right on the other side of that mountain." Once he got us so lost I resorted to firing three shots in rapid succession. But the light was bad and I missed him.

Dear PFM:

The other fellows in my hunting camp sit around each evening sipping whiskey, chawing on tobacco, and telling coarse jokes. I have never done any of these things. Naturally, I don't want to offend my friends, but what can I do?

Pure in Pasadena

Dear Pure:

This is a very delicate matter and you must treat it as such. Sipping whiskey while chawing tobacco and telling jokes can be downright disgusting if not done properly, and I can understand how you might disgust your friends if you're just a beginner. I suggest you practice at home behind the garage until you get the technique down.

Dear PFM:

A member of our hunting party volunteered one freezing morning to get up and build the morning campfire. As he stepped out onto the frosted ground barefoot and wearing only his longjohns, he spotted a buck deer crossing a clearing up on the mountain. Snatching up his rifle, he charged off after the buck. Several hours later he returned to camp, dragging the deer. His underwear was torn and filthy. Although his feet were half frozen, he danced around camp laughing and joking and telling us about how he had tracked down the deer. Is this abnormal behavior for a hunter? What is the proper thing for us to do?

Concerned in Cody

Dear Con:

This is the most serious case I've heard about in years. Anyone who volunteers to get up and build the morning campfire has to be crazy! Encourage him to seek professional help, particularly if you notice any other odd behavior on his part.

Dear PFM:

A friend of mine recently stunned a large buck with his last shell. As Joe approached the fallen animal intending to finish it off with his knife, the deer staggered to its feet and began wobbling up a hill. Joe grabbed the buck by the tail and tried to pull it back down. The deer, however, began not only to recover its senses but to pick up speed, and soon it was fairly flying up the hill with Joe hanging on to its tail. As they topped the hill, they practically trampled a young hunter by the name of Rich, also from our camp, who had just come up the hill from the far side. At that moment, Joe let go of the deer's tail, did a couple of somersaults, sat up, shook his head in disgust, and thrust the knife back into its sheath. "Dang," he said to young Rich, "I'm just getting too old to run deer down with a knife. From now on I'm goin' to use a rifle!" My question is, do you think if we told young Rich the truth, it would help him recover, or should we just let him continue to stare off into space?

Sincere in Cincinnati

Dear Sin:

This is an extremely dangerous situation. I have heard that story told at least five hundred times in hunting camps, and the next person who tries to tell it will be sealed in his sleeping bag and freeze-dried as a warning to others.

Dear PFM:

I pulled this practical joke on my hunting companions. After they had gone to sleep and the fire was out, I filled their rubber boots full of water. The next morning they jumped out of bed to go duck hunting and their boots were solid ice. Ha ha! Since mine were the only boots without ice in them, they knew who had pulled the joke on them. Ha ha! I will be out of the hospital soon and want to know if I did anything wrong when I pulled this joke on my former buddies.

Jokester in Jersey

Dear Joke:

You most certainly did do something wrong! Anyone who pulls a great practical joke like that should be smart enough to sleep with his boots on.

Dear PFM:

Some of the guys want you to settle an argument: Which is proper to use with camp meals, paper or cloth napkins?

Also, should dishes be passed left to right or right to left? And finally, should the salad fork or the cocktail fork be placed next to the dinner fork?

Mannerly in Missoula

Dear Man:

Every time somebody sets up a new hunting camp, these same questions arise, and I am sick and tired of answering them! For the last time: cloth, left to right, and salad!

Dear PFM:

We recently discovered an abandoned hunting camp, complete with a big old log cabin, which we have fixed up. The hunters who owned the cabin disappeared rather mysteriously, or so we are told by some of the locals. What bothers us, though, is we think the cabin is haunted. In the middle of the night we hear this strange moaning in the room. Then a quavering voice repeats over and over again, "Don't eat the stew! Don't eat the stew!" What do you think it means?

Fearful in Fargo

Dear Fearful:

Don't eat the stew, dummy.

Stone Soup

Early one summer morning, Crazy Eddie Muldoon stopped by my house and told me he was running away from home. "Want to come along?" he asked.

I was out feeding the chickens at the time. When you're eight years old, feeding chickens can be complicated. On this particular morning it had been necessary for me to scratch a huge smiling face in the dirt with a stick and then carefully pour wheat along the lines before letting the chickens out of their house. Crazy Eddie seemed unaware that he was standing right next to a living, scratching, pecking work of art, a smiling face composed entirely of live chickens.

"How come you're running away?" I asked.

"My folks work me too hard," he said. "I'm fed up."

Offhand, I could not remember ever seeing Eddie do any work for his folks, but maybe they worked him nights, when I wasn't around.

"Mine too," I said. "You see these chickens? It must have taken me an hour to feed them this morning."

Eddie tossed the hair back out of his eyes, still ignoring the chicken face. "Well, you want to run away?"

Lacking any other plans for the day, I said, "Okay, when do we leave?"

"Right now," Eddie said.

"I can't go right now," I said. "I've got to eat breakfast and clean my room first."

"Well, hurry," Eddie said.

"I'll get my mom to make us a lunch while I'm cleaning my room," I said.

"Don't do that," Eddie said, his freckles merging into an expression of disgust. "You can't have your mom make a lunch. You have to sneak the food. Don't you know anything about running away?"

"This is my first time," I said. "I'll try to sneak some food."

"Good," Eddie said. "I brought along a gunnysack to carry our food and stuff in. Now hurry. And don't get caught."

Don't get caught! What a wonderful expression! If there was one thing Eddie knew how to do, it was to charge me up for a new adventure.

My mother was in the kitchen clearing away the breakfast dishes when I rushed in. I snatched a couple of pieces of cold toast and a strip of bacon off a moving plate.

"You made it just in time, buster," she said. "Land sakes, I never knew anybody to take so long to feed chickens! Now go clean up your room. Smells like something died in there!"

Actually, it had died on the highway, squashed flat by a big truck, but this was no time to argue fine points. I waited until Mom left the kitchen, then sneaked as much food as I could cram into a paper sack and took off.

Crazy Eddie was waiting out behind the woodshed. "That was fast," he said.

"Yeah," I said. "I didn't clean my room. I figured what's the use cleaning my room if I'm running away."

"I wondered about that," Eddie said. "You're starting to catch on."

I put my paper bag of sneaked food into our pack. Eddie swung the gunnysack over his shoulder, staggered back a few steps, caught his balance, and then started off in the direction of the creek.

"Where we running away to?" I asked.

"Well, the first thing, we got to wade up the crick to the railroad bridge."

"How come we got to wade up the crick?"

" 'Cause that's the way it's done, don't you know that? It's so the sheriff and the posse can't follow your trail."

"Hold up a sec, Eddie," I said, my tennis shoes squeaking on the grass as I slid to a stop. "Tell me that again about the sheriff and the posse."

"They always send the sheriff and the posse after runaways," he said. "But don't worry. By the time they find out we're gone, we'll be so far away they'll never catch us."

"How are we going to get so far away?"

"We'll hop a freight."

Amazing! After all the wild and ridiculous ideas Crazy Eddie had come up with that summer, he had finally hit on something sensible. He went on to explain how we would become hoboes and ride freights all over the country and camp out under the stars. After our food ran out, he said, we would live off the land, picking wild berries and catching fish and stuff.

"Which reminds me," he said. "What kind of food did you sneak?"

"Let's see, I got half a box of cornflakes, a jar of milk and some sugar to eat on the cornflakes, a can of pork 'n' beans, four pieces of fried chicken, half a loaf of bread, a jar of jam, a bunch of carrots, about a dozen sugar cookies, some raisins, three apples, and a package of graham crackers." I could tell from the expression on Eddie's face that he disapproved of my selection.

"What'd you bring carrots for?" he said. "They're one of the reasons I'm running away."

We waded up the creek toward the railroad bridge, the water reaching only slightly above our ankles but still deep enough to throw the sheriff and the posse off our trail. Some of the families who lived along the creek used it for a dump. This was back in the days before we had either ecology or environment, and creeks were often regarded as good garbage collectors. Eddie and I sorted through several dumps and found an old kettle and a few other odds and ends to use on our adventure. We added the new finds to the gunnysack, under the weight of which we took turns staggering along toward the railroad bridge. Running away had turned out to be much harder work than I expected.

We reached the railroad bridge about noon and were surprised to see two men sitting in the shade beneath it. They had built a fire and were roasting a chunk of baloney on the end of a sharpened stick. Both of them were gazing at the sizzling meat as if it were the most fascinating thing they had ever seen. Then they noticed us.

I whispered to Eddie, "What'll we do?"

"They're hoboes," he said out of the corner of his mouth. "Real hoboes. Maybe they'll want to talk to us."

"Maybe they'll want to murder us," I said, lacking Crazy Eddie's natural optimism. I lowered the gunnysack to a sandbar, looked around for an escape route, and began silently to rev my internal-combustion engine.

One of the men had dirty white hair reaching nearly to

his shoulders. He beckoned to us with a long, bony finger.

"It's okay," Eddie said. "Look. They're smiling."

Well, that was a relief! I hoisted the sack back onto my shoulder and we slogged up the creek to the bridge.

"Howdy," Eddie said.

"Howdy," the white-haired man said. "What you boys doin' out here?"

"We're running away," said Eddie. "Gonna be hoboes and ride freight trains around the country."

The man nodded, still smiling broadly. "Runnin' away," he said. "Gonna be hoboes. Hmmmmm. Maybe Wild Bill and me can show you a few of the ropes. This here's Wild Bill. I'm Whitey. Me and Bill been hoboin' a long time, ain't that right, Bill?"

"Yep," Wild Bill said. He was tall and gangly, with black hair and a big mustache that curled up on the ends. He didn't seem nearly so friendly as Whitey. "Whatcha got in the gunnysack, kid?" he said to me.

"Nothing much," I said. "Just some food."

Wild Bill and Whitey both stared at the sack as though it were an unexpected birthday present.

"What kind of food?" Whitey said, leaning forward.

Pleased by their obvious interest, I reached in the sack and pulled out the first thing I could find.

Wild Bill and Whitey seemed to sag. "Carrots," Bill said. "Cripes, that's why I run away from home myself."

I tossed the carrots in the creek and began to haul out, one by one, each item of our food supply. With the appearance of each new course, Bill and Whitey *ooh*ed and *aah*ed as if they were watching a Fourth of July fireworks display. In addition to my sneaked food, Eddie had sneaked a chunk of roast beef, a slice of fried ham, three wieners, some cheese, an onion, several quart jars of fruit, a jar of dill pickles, and a jar of canned rabbit. As I arranged the food in neat rows along the bank, Wild Bill and Whitey looked as if they were about to cry.

"I told you there was a God," Whitey said to Bill.

Why Wild Bill might have had any doubt, I couldn't imagine. Of course there was a God. Everybody knew that. Where did Bill think babies came from?

"Boys," Whitey said, "we was just fixin' a bite to eat." He pointed at the blackened chunk of baloney on the end of the stick. "Care to join us?"

"Naw," Eddie said. "You don't have enough. Pat and me will just eat some of our own food."

One entire side of Wild Bill's face twitched. "You don't seem to get the pitcher, kid," he said, with possibly a hint of menace.

"Ha ha," Whitey laughed. "You see, the first thing you got to learn about hoboin' is that when a bunch of us hoboes gets together, we always share whatever food anybody's brought. It's only polite, and that way the hoboes what don't have much food, they don't try to kil . . . uh, don't get peeved at you for not mindin' your manners."

"Oh," Eddie said. "In that case, we'll share our food. We've only been hoboin' for a few hours and didn't know."

"That's all right," Whitey said, as he and Bill each grabbed chicken drumsticks and sucked them to the bare bone in a single slurp. Then they snatched up the rest of the chicken and repeated the performance. Whitey wiped his mouth on his sleeve and rolled his eyes, pretending those old cold pieces of chicken were about the best thing he had ever tasted in his life. Eddie and I laughed appreciatively at their clowning.

Wild Bill now seemed to be in a better humor. "Say, Whitey, maybe we should make the boys some soup. We can heat up this canned rabbit for ourselves and they can eat the soup."

"Good idea," Whitey said. "You boys like soup?"

"What kind of soup?"

"Hobo soup. It's made with a soup stone."

"I never heard of a soup stone," I said. "What does it taste like?"

"Any flavor you like. All us hoboes carry a soup stone. When a hobo ain't got nothin' else to eat, he gets out his soup stone and boils it in a pot of water, with a little salt and pepper."

"Hey, yeah," Eddie said. "We'd like to try that. Where do you get these soup stones, anyway?"

"Mexico," Bill said. "They're kind of expensive, but you boys get to hoboin' down that way, you want to pick up one. You got the soup stone, Whitey?"

"I left it down here by the crick," Whitey said. "Ah, here it is." He bent over and picked up a gray, rounded stone. You had to look at it pretty carefully to see that it wasn't just an ordinary old gray rock, but the way Whitey handled it, you could tell the stone was precious. He placed it gently in the bottom of a tin can, scooped the can full of water from the creek, and set it over the fire.

While our soup and their rabbit were warming over the fire, Whitey and Wild Bill entertained us by eating our food in a comical manner. Bill slurped down a whole jar of peaches without even taking a breath, while Whitey hacked off two thick slabs of bread and made himself a sandwich that must have weighed nine pounds. The rabbit had only heated to about lukewarm before they devoured it. Then they lay back burping and groaning happily to watch Eddie and me eat our soup.

"How's the soup?" Whitey asked.

I smiled and smacked my lips politely. "Real good."

"I think it needs a little salt," Eddie said.

"Believe me, it tastes a whole lot better after you been hoboin' awhile," Whitey said.

"You bet," Wild Bill said, massaging his belly.

"Say, you were going to teach us the ropes about hoboin'," Eddie said.

"Oh, yeah, that's right," said Whitey. "Well, it's pretty exciting, particularly at night in the boxcars. That's when the big hairy spiders come out. They're about this big." He put his hairy hand down clawlike on the ground and made a scrabbling motion with it toward Eddie and me. We jumped back, almost spilling our soup. Wild Bill and Whitey chuckled.

"Tell 'em about Hatchet Harvey and how he killed them two young fellas to get their soup stone," Wild Bill said.

"Not while they're still eatin' their soup," Whitey said. "I don't want to spoil their appetites. Youngsters need lots of nourishment. But look here at this, boys." He rolled up one of his dirt-caked pantlegs and showed us a huge, horrible, appetite-spoiling sore on his leg. "Just look at this. One of them big ol' hairy spiders did it to me. Oh, it hurt like blazes, and I was howlin' and screamin' and tryin' to pull that ol' spider off, but he had his ugly jaws clamped on to my leg right down into the meat and was shootin' his poison in . . ."

A couple of hours later, Crazy Eddie and I were poking along the road that led back to our homes, Eddie having decided it would be better to postpone running away until after his birthday the following month.

"You think that was true, what Whitey told about the spider?" he asked.

"Naw," I said. "He was just tryin' to scare us."

"That's what I thought, too," Eddie said. "Both Wild Bill and Whitey must be pretty dumb to think we'd believe those stories."

"Of course they're dumb," I said. "Why else would they let us trade them the rest of our food for their soup stone?"

Gunrunning

Hubert, a young married fellow of my acquaintance, confided in me the other day that he and his wife had just had their first quarrel.

"Oh, yeah?" I said. "What about?"

"About practically nothing," he said. "I've been needing a new rifle, so I went out and bought one and took it home to show Joyce. Well, if she didn't hit the ceiling! Mad? Whew! Can you believe it?"

"That was dumb, Hubie," I said. "Risking your marriage over a new gun. I thought you were smarter than that."

"I shouldn't have bought the gun, huh?"

"Of course you should have bought the gun. You needed it, didn't you? You just shouldn't have shown the gun to Joyce. Have a little consideration for her feelings, Hubie. Wives have feelings too, you know. The only decent thing for a husband to do is to sneak the new gun into the house. Learn to sneak, man, learn to sneak."

"Really?" Hubie said. "I didn't know."

During my talk with Hubie, it occurred to me that there are probably many other young married hunters out there who are equally in need of marriage counseling. In the interest of averting as much marital discord in the hunting fraternity as possible, I have put together the following primer on strategies and tactics for bringing home a new gun.

First of all, let us consider the psychology of the young wife as it pertains to her husband's guns. It is important to note that the first gun the husband brings home is greeted with considerable enthusiasm by the spouse, and she may even brag about it to her friends. "Fred bought a new gun the other day to hunt elk and doves and things with," she will say. Of course, Fred must then explain that the gun is limited to hunting elk or deer. For hunting doves he needs a shotgun, he tells her.

"Why can't you hunt doves with the same gun?" she says. "I really think you could if you wanted to."

Fred then explains the difference between a rifle and a shotgun, and his wife finally agrees that he probably does need another gun.

Now that's the typical situation the young hunter faces. He starts with a base of two guns, his wife granting him the benefit of the doubt that two guns are actually needed. After the second gun, the argument that he *needs* a new gun will be dismissed by the wife with an upward roll of the eyeballs and a big sigh. We are talking only third gun here, remember, nothing more. If you're just married, upward-rolling eyeballs and big sighs may seem formidable obstacles, but they're really not that serious. Go buy the gun and bring it home. The eyeball-rolling and big sighs will let up after a few days. Now comes the biggie—the Fourth Gun!

With the mere mention of your need for a fourth gun, the wife skips right over the eyeball-rolling and big sighs and goes directly to a recital of your deficiencies of character, weird masculine quirks, and all sins committed to date. She will bring up such matters as saving for the baby's college education, the fact that she is still wearing the clothes her parents bought her in high school, the threatening note from the electric company, etc. "And you want another gun!" she will finish, the sarcasm flickering about the room like sheet lightning.

The fourth gun is the tough one, and in the face of this spousal assault, there is always the temptation to sneak the fourth gun. That's a mistake. Your wife's knowing you purchased a fourth gun is essential to further development of your gun collection. Here's why. After you bring the gun home and show it to your wife, she will shake her head and say, "I don't know why you need all those guns." Note that she doesn't say "four guns" but rather the vague and general "all those guns." Henceforth, she will think of your gun collection not in terms of specific numbers but as a single collective entity—all!

To thoroughly grasp this important concept, suppose your wife is dusting the gun case. "Him and all those guns," she might say to herself, possibly with a very tiny tolerant smile. What she fails to notice is that there are now *five* guns in the case! Once the psychological barrier of the fourth gun is crossed, the gun collection can be expanded indefinitely without the wife's noticing, provided the husband uses some common sense and doesn't add too many guns at once. Two or three a year is about right, spaced at decent intervals.

There is one pitfall in this strategy—the gun cabinet itself. Although the wife will never bother to count the guns, she will notice that there are three empty slots in the cabinet. Therefore, you must make sure that there are always three empty slots in the cabinet, even as your collection expands from four to sixty guns. If you plan on enlarging your collection, buy a gun cabinet that can be expanded by adding new sections, so that there are always three or more empty slots. It works. My wife of thirty years told me the other day that she must be slowing down with age. "When we were first married," she said, "I could dust that gun cabinet of yours in ten seconds and now it takes me nearly half an hour."

But how do you get all those guns into the house without your wife's knowing, you ask. Actually, it is all right if every few years you simply walk right into the house and say, "Look, dear, I bought a new gun."

"Neato," she will say. "I'm ecstatic. Now tell me, what did you want to buy another gun for when you already have all those guns? I'll bet you haven't shot most of them in the past five years."

Shot them? Yes, a wife will actually say that. She will not be able to comprehend that you needed the gun because you needed it. She will not understand that you need the guns just to be there, to be *your* guns, to be looked at and fondled from time to time. She will not be able to fathom that you need the guns even though you don't need to shoot them. Tell her a gun collection is like wilderness. Even though we don't use all of it all the time, we need to know it's there. Probably it won't do any good to tell her that, but it's worth a try.

Stating the simple truth often works in explaining an occasional gun purchase to your wife. But why take unnecessary risks? Go with your best lie and get the gun stashed in your expandable gun cabinet as quickly as possible.

Oddly enough, there are few really good lies for explaining the purchase of a new gun. There's the classic "A Fantastic Bargain," of course, in which you tell your wife that the gun you just paid $300 for was on sale for $27.50. If her eyebrows shoot up in disbelief, you mention that three men in white coats showed up at the sport shop and led the manager away before he could slash the prices on the rest of the guns. Indeed, you say, you could have picked up five more brand-new guns for a total of eighty-five dollars, but you didn't want to take excessive advantage of a crazy person.

The "Play on Her Sympathy Ploy" works well on young, inexperienced wives. It goes something like this: Rush into the house wiping tears of joy from your cheeks. Then cry out, "Look, Martha, look! A man at the garage sold me this rifle. It's identical to the one my grandfather gave me on his deathbed. Gramps said to me, 'Boy, I'm givin' you ol' Betsy here, because every time you shoot it, you will remember all the good times you and me had together.' Oh, how I hated to sell that rifle to pay for Momma's operation! But now I got one just like it! Or maybe it's even the same rifle! Do you think it might actually be the same rifle, Martha?"

Warning! Don't ever try the Sympathy Ploy on a wife you've been married to for longer than five years, unless you want to see a woman laugh herself sick. It's a disgusting spectacle, I can tell you.

The "Fantastic Investment" lie will work on occasion, provided you lay the groundwork carefully in advance. "That ol' Harvey Schmartz is a shrewd one," you say. "He bought this .48-caliber Thumblicker for six hundred dollars as an investment. Three weeks later he sold it for eighty-seven thousand dollars! Boy, I wish I could lay my hands on a .48-caliber Thumblicker. We'd sell it when I retire and buy us a condo in Aspen and tour Europe with the change."

After you've used up all your best lies, you are left with

only one option. You must finally screw up your courage, square your jaw, and make up your mind that you are going to do what you probably should have done all along—sneak the new guns into the house.

Here are some proven techniques for gun-sneaking:

The Surprise Party—You arrive home and tell your wife that you have to go to a surprise birthday party for one of your hunting partners and picked up the special cake on your way home. "Oh, how cute!" she will exclaim. "A birthday cake shaped like a rifle!" This is also known as "The Gun-in-Cake Trick."

The Lamp—You buy a lampshade and attach it to the muzzle of a new rifle. "Look, sweetheart," you say to your spouse. "I bought a new lamp for the living room." She gags. "Not for my living room," she growls. "Take it to your den and don't ever let me see that monstrosity again!" A variation on this ploy is to tie a picture wire to the new rifle and call it a wall hanging.

The Loan—A hunting friend shows up at your door and hands you your new gun. "Thanks for loaning me one of your rifles," he says. "I'll do the same for you sometime." Make sure your accomplice can be trusted, though. I tried "The Loan" with Retch Sweeney one time and he didn't show up at my door with the rifle for three weeks, on the day after hunting season, as I recall.

Spare Parts—Disassemble the gun and carry it home in a shopping bag. Mention casually to the Mrs. that you picked up some odds and ends from the junk bin down at Joe's Gunsmithing. Works like a charm! (By the way, does anyone know where the little wishbone-shaped gizmo goes in an automatic shotgun?)

The Wager

It's no secret that everyone I go fishing with catches more fish than I do. (I have tried to keep it a secret, but that's impossible when you fish only with a bunch of blabbermouths.) The true reason I catch so few fish is that I am a conservationist. My fishing partners refuse to accept this true reason. They say the actual true reason I catch so few fish is my lousy casting, which they compare to the technique of an old woman beating out a rug with a broomstick. Little do they know how difficult it is for a person possessed of my mastery of fishing to feign lousy casting technique in the interest of conservation.

I am reminded of a fishing trip I went on with Dave Lisaius and Jim Abrahamson, which isn't too difficult to be reminded of, since it took place just last week. Dave and Jim may leap to the conclusion that I am reminded of the trip merely in retaliation for the unmerciful ridicule they directed at my apparent inability to catch more than two fish a day. Nothing could be further from the truth. I bring up the fishing trip only for the purpose of illustrating certain ethical, psychological, sociological, and economic concepts. So there!

I will not mention the name of the lake here, because then thousands of anglers would descend upon it, thereby enriching the resort owner, whose wife, joining in the fun over my take of two measly fish a day, told me her secret to catching the really big ones was to bait the hook with a piece of Bit-O-Honey candy bar. Ha! She probably thought I was dumb enough to fall for that one, particularly since I was fishing with two weird guys like Jim and Dave. If there's one thing I'm not, it's gullible, no matter what my mother goes around telling people.

On the morning of the third day of the trip, I arose in my typically responsible manner and went outside to chop kindling and firewood to build a fire in the stove of our rustic cabin. As soon as the fire was crackling, the coffee perking, and the bacon sputtering, I detected for the first time in eight hours a pause in the thunderous din that Jim modestly refers to as his "snoring." (Upon hearing his first snore from the loft above me, I mistook it for the sound of huge claws ripping shingles from the roof. I was much relieved to learn it was only Jim's snores ripping shingles from the roof.) Jim soon descended the stairs from the loft, scratching and grumbling, and asking what's for breakfast. He quickly wolfed down a slab of huckleberry pie, dribbling the juice down the front of his long underwear until he looked like a victim in a horror movie. (This mention of his uncouth eating habits serves only to illustrate a sociological concept. It in no way relates to the abominable delight Jim displayed over my failing to catch more than two fish a day.)

The spectacle of Dave's arising in the morning provokes

such queasiness among even hardened observers that my
editor has asked me to delete the description of it in the
interest of good taste. I will mention, however, that Dave
claims his new sleeping bag came equipped with a ther-
mostatically controlled zipper that allows him to emerge from
the bag only after the surrounding temperature reaches
seventy-two degrees. It looks like an ordinary zipper to
me, but every time I mention it, Dave launches into a long
speech about the marvels of technological miniaturization.
To test the zipper, I tape-recorded the sounds of a fire
crackling, bacon frying, and coffee perking. Although I
haven't tried out the recording yet, I am reasonably sure
it will trip the zipper on Dave's sleeping bag on even a subzero morning, the marvels of technological miniaturization
notwithstanding.

Dave was in his usual ghastly good humor.

"Boy, are my arms ever sore from fighting big rainbows
all day," he said to me. "You're sure lucky you don't have
to put up with this kind of suffering." Then he began emit-
ting the sharp little barks that after some study I have identified as his laugh.

"Hmmmph!" I shot back. (My well-known facility for
repartee seldom peaks before noon.)

Jim began talking with his mouth full. "You know what?
I think we should do something to make today's fishing more
interesting for ol' Pat. It can't be much fun for him, sitting
in the boat all day watching us catch fish." Here he erupted
into an explosion of mirth that splattered two walls of the
cabin with chewed morsels of food. I was glad he had previously finished with the huckleberry pie. Otherwise, future
renters of the cabin might easily have supposed an ax murder had taken place there.

"Good idea," said Dave, trying to scratch between his

shoulder blades with a table fork. "I think we should work out a little wager, where the guy who catches the fewest fish pays each of the other two guys one dollar for each fish they catch more than he does."

"I like it!" cried Jim. "But why not make it five dollars per fish?"

I shook my head in disgust. "That's a terrible idea," I said. "Do you know what you are suggesting?"

"Yup," said Dave. "A way to buy a new graphite rod I've been looking at."

"Not at all," I said. "You are suggesting that we reduce the pure sport of fishing to nothing more than a stupid, mundane game upon which to bet, like golf! Besides, the whole idea violates my conservation ethic."

The two of them sat there with egg on their faces. How they had managed that with hard-boiled eggs, I don't know.

"Yeah, you're right," said Jim. "I certainly wouldn't want to do anything that contributes to fishing gluttony."

"Me neither," said Dave. "So suppose we bet one dollar on catching the first fish and five dollars on the biggest fish."

"Great!" said Jim. "That will keep Pat's interest up, and he won't pout all day. But why don't we make it seven-fifty for the biggest fish?"

"We're not having any ridiculous bets like seven-fifty," Dave said sternly. "We'll make it ten for the first fish and another ten for the biggest fish."

"Okay, you're on," I said.

Dave and Jim clapped their hands in glee, putting me in mind of preschoolers who have just been told to expect a surprise. (Once again, I mention these peculiar idiosyncrasies of my companions only for the purpose of illustrating certain psychological concepts and not because of their disgusting merriment over my catching only two fish a day.)

After breakfast, I washed the dishes and tidied up the cabin, while Jim and Dave studied the fishing regulations pamphlet. They did much better than on the previous day, and I only had to help them sound out four or five of the longer words. As soon as the lesson was over, we headed for the lake.

I had promised the guys that they could back the trailer into the water and launch the boat themselves.

"Now don't tell us anything," Dave said. "We want to do it all by ourselves."

I didn't say a word, and presently we were in the boat, churning our way up the lake.

"Seems to be a bit sluggish," Dave said.

"Yeah," said Jim.

"Want me to tell you why?" I asked.

"Oh, all right," Dave said.

"You're supposed to take the boat off the trailer."

Both Dave and Jim are banking executives, and I suppose they can't be expected to know about boats too. Still, I could not help wondering whether there might not be an inverse ratio between intelligence and blabbing all over town about how many more fish they catch than I do.

When my competitors weren't watching, I baited up with my new miracle fish-attractor. After an hour without a single strike, it became clear to me that the new miracle fish-attractor was a total flop. Fortunately, Dave and Jim hadn't got a nibble yet either, so I was still in the running for first fish.

"Either of you guys want the rest of this?" I asked amiably, indicating the new miracle fish-attractor.

"Sure," said Jim. "I love Bit-O-Honey candy bars. How come you brought it along if you don't want to eat it?"

I gave him my inscrutable smile and tied on a pink lure.

A few minutes later my rod whipped down and the reel began singing like a goosed soprano. I boated THE FIRST FISH OF THE DAY.

Jim and Dave turned glum. I don't know whether it was because they thought I had already won the wagers for both the first fish and the biggest fish or because they were worried that my dancing an Irish jig would capsize the boat.

Several times during the day, both Dave and Jim hooked fish that might have been larger than mine, but when I attempted to net the thrashing lunkers for them, the fish managed to wrap the line around the net handle and get away. Naturally, the lads both screamed at me on these occasions, even though I explained that it is not unusual for an angler, caught up in the excitement of netting one of his competitors' fish, to dip the net in the water handle-first.

Toward the end of the day I could tell that Dave and Jim were getting nervous about the wager, when they began discussing its terms.

"Let's see, the largest fish was seven-fifty, wasn't it?" Jim said.

"I recall five," Dave said. "Remember, you said let's make it seven-fifty and I said, no, five is enough."

"I remember ten bucks for the biggest fish," I said. "And furthermore, when we were discussing the bet, I made a tape recording of our conversation."

"You did?" Dave said. "Why, that's the most dishonorable thing I've ever heard of!"

"Right," I said, taking the recorder from my pocket. "Now let me play back to you the exact terms of the bet."

They listened to the recording for a few seconds, becoming increasingly puzzled.

"Sounds to me like a fire crackling, bacon frying, and coffee perking," Dave said.

"Wrong recording," I said.

As it turned out, the recorder had malfunctioned during the discussion over the terms of the bet, and I had to settle for $7.50 for FIRST FISH, plus another $7.50 for ***!!**LARGEST FISH**!!***, although I would be loath to call attention to the fact that my first fish was also largest of the day.

Dave and Jim were so upset over my winning the wager that they could scarcely wait to get back to town and begin regaling our mutual acquaintances with comic descriptions of my catching only two fish a day. Which reminds me of some of their other bad habits, strange behavior, and loathsome table manners. One night when I was pleading with them not to go carousing in sleazy bars . . .

Letters from Camp

I have recently come into possession of some letters from camp. They were written by my next-door neighbor, Fenton Quagmire, during the course of a hunting trip he, Retch Sweeney, and I took to Montana a few years ago. The letters, written to Quagmire's wife, Marge, are of interest for a number of reasons. First of all, they show a childish and peevish man growing quickly to maturity as a result of enduring the hardships of his first hunting trip. Second, the letters were introduced as evidence in two lawsuits, one a divorce case that Mrs. Quagmire brought against her husband, and the other an alienation-of-affection case she filed against Sweeney and me. I am happy to report that Marge eventually regained possession of her senses and withdrew both suits. In fact, it was she who gave me the letters, along with some blunt advice as to their disposition. I thought the advice a bit extreme, if not unladylike, and have chosen instead to publish the letters here in the hope that they will show the therapeutic effects of a simple hunting trip.

Saturday, 12:30 p.m.

My Dearest Darling Dumpling,

Am writing these letters to you in case I don't survive this trip with the two madmen and so you will have something to remember me by.

Have stopped briefly in middle of a godforsaken prairie here in Montana. The two madmen, McManus and Sweeney, have got out of car to settle dispute between them. Sweeney claims Indians used to attract buffalo within range of arrows by waving white flag. McManus argues trick was used on antelope. Small herd of buffalo near highway, and McManus is standing out there laughing uproariously, as is his fashion, while Sweeney waves T-shirt at buffalo.

Why I ever let them talk me into this trip I'll never know. To think that I'll be in their company for another whole week is almost more than I can stand. Must admit, however, that so far trip has exceeded my wildest expectations, which is to say that I am still alive and unmaimed and if I ever ge

Saturday, 3:30 p.m.

Back again, Dearest Darling Dumpling,

McManus peeved and even more sarcastic than usual, if you can imagine. Asked him straight out, would he rather cling with his fingers to rain gutter of station wagon for few hundred yards at high speed or have both vehicle *and himself* wiped out in buffalo stampede? Just fortunate for all concerned I had presence of mind to throw wagon in gear and stomp on accelerator. You'd have been proud of Hubby-Wubby!

As yet no sign of Sweeney. Have told McManus to calm down, not to worry. When Sweeney went over top of hill he had good lead on buffalo. Don't know how interested you are in buffalo lore, but their curiosity is aroused by waving white T-shirt.

Your Hubby-Wubby

Saturday, 5:30 p.m.

Dearest Darling Dumpling,

Back again.

Have left prairie behind and moving up into mountains. Scenery absolutely splendid. Peaks frosted with snow, foothills ablaze with color—chokecherry, birch, alder, quaking aspen. Which reminds me—Sweeney back with us again and none the worse for wear. Looks better for having shed a few pounds. Managed to run in a wide circle and, as I anticipated, we intercepted him as he crossed highway, although not until second time around. Buffalo exhausted. Sweeney recuperating fast, to judge from his determined but feeble attempts to reach up and squeeze my throat. Sweeney great clown! Such crude humor, tho, not to my taste.

Should make camp soon. Will try to add note to this letter before we hit goosedown.

Love, Hubby-Wubby

Saturday, 9:30 p.m.

Dearest Darling Dumpling,

At my wits' end! Oh, how I long to be curled up beside you under our dual-control queen-sized electric blanket! These imbeciles! These morons! Cannot believe what they perpetrated against me. One of the fatheads forgot his sleeping bag! Neither, of course, will admit to being the villain.

Even tried to make out it was *I* who forgot *my* sleeping bag. What they have suggested—no, in fact demanded—is we zip the two sleeping bags together and all three of us sleep in the communal bag! Can you imagine such a disgusting thing? Have told them I will sit outside tent all night by fire, rather than submit to gross indignity of such arrangement.

Your Hubby-Wubby, Fenton

Sunday, 10:00 a.m.

My Dearest Darling Dumpling,

Place where we're camped very wild, apparently inhabited by sizable population of grizzly bears. Last night one started howling short distance from camp. McManus identified the hideous wailing as that of grizzly. Still shudder when I think of it. Am exhausted, having got almost no sleep last night. Have you ever slept in a double sleeping bag with two men who snore? No, I suppose not. Most uncomfortable and distasteful, particularly when you are in the middle and other two have been chased by buffalo earlier in day.

Food terrible. McManus whipped up his infamous Watchagot stew for supper last night. We ate it in pitch darkness, the only redeeming feature of meal. Coffee tasted like boiled socks, biscuits had to be cracked with hatchet. Whipped topping McManus sprayed on instant dessert turned out to be my shaving cream. Ate only the shaving cream since didn't trust dessert. Must run now.

Your ever-loving Hubby-Wubby

Sunday, 7:00 p.m.

Dearest Darling Dumpling,

Today uneventful. Went on first hunt. Sport highly overrated. Meatheads took me out to a cleared area and told me to watch it while they circled around mountain and "drove" toward me. Nothing more boring than watching a clearing, unless perhaps it is listening to McManus reminisce interminably about his childhood.

Finally, out of boredom and for joke, made huge grizzly track in soft dirt, left my hat on ground a few yards away, then went back to camp and caught some shut-eye in communal sleeping bag. Must have been exhausted because didn't wake up until heard McManus & Sweeney talking outside tent. You would have laughed!

"Poor Quagmire," McManus said.

"Yep," said Sweeney, "he was nice little guy."

"You think a grizzly got him?"

"Maybe. Never seen a grizzly track that big before—eighteen claws!"

"We're going to have to tell his wife what happened to him. Now don't let me forget!"

"I won't. She's probably going to be upset."

"Probably. You know what this means, don't you?"

"Yeah. We can each have our own sleeping bag tonight."

Fearing they would turn maudlin, I leaped out of tent and yelled, "Surprise! I'm alive!"

"We thought you got et," was all Sweeney could bring himself to say.

McManus struggled to control his emotions. "Anyway, tonight's my turn to sleep in the middle," he said.

Sort of moved by their reaction. Hadn't realized they liked me.

Love, Hubby-Wubby

Monday

Dearest Darling Dumpling,
   McManus & Sweeney teaching me all kinds of good stuff about hunting and camping. Let me build campfire this morning. Rather amusing, since both wanted to build it. After brief argument, McManus said, "Heck, why don't we let Quagmire build the fire? It's not fair for you and me to hog all the fun."
   "Yeah, I guess you're right," Sweeney said. "Fenton, you get to build the fire."
   Building campfire isn't as easy as you might think. First had to knock all the snow off the firewood. Nearly froze to death before I got fire going. But it was worth it. McManus & Sweeney came out of tent later and critiqued fire.
   "Not a bad fire for your first time," McManus told me.
   "Yeah, you done good, Fent," Sweeney said.
   "All he needs is just a bit more practice to get his fire-building technique perfected, don't you think, Retch?"
   "Maybe we should let him get up and build the fire every morning," Sweeney said.
   "Yeah, I suppose you're right."
   Then they made me the official firebuilder! It's quite an honor.
   Know it sounds crazy, but can't tell you how pleased I am that they would entrust me with this important chore. They even talk about letting me make the coffee in the morning! Which reminds me, Sweeney found the sock he lost. Coffee has since improved.
   Now for the best news. Sweeney shot nice buck today; and I nearly shot one! Herd of deer came right by me. Slipped rifle safety off and aimed just behind shoulder of

big buck, held breath, and slowly squeezed trigger, just like McManus showed me. He watched through binoculars and said later I did everything just right! Said he is really pleased the way I handled myself.

"Starting tomorrow, Fenton," he told me, "you get to put shells in your rifle." Can hardly wait!

Love, Hubby

Thursday

Dear Dumpling,

You're not going to believe this, but I'm now official camp cook. Pat and Retch say they've never seen anybody catch on to hunting camp routine so fast.

Turns out that I'm a surprisingly good shot. Got two grouse today with my rifle and cooked them for supper. Wrapped them in aluminum foil with a bit of bacon and baked them in coals. Pat said they were almost as good as his Whatchagot stew, which is great compliment from him. For breakfast tomorrow I'm cooking pancakes and venison steaks. Pat and Retch have offered to do dishes, clean my rifle, and oil my boots.

Love, Hub

Friday

Dear Dump,

Good ol' Pat got his deer today, a four-point mulie. Even asked my advice, if you can imagine that. Told him I figured deer would be bedded down on the leeward side of the ridge because a sharp wind blowing all morning. Told him I'd swing around on the downwind side and see if I couldn't flush deer out onto open ground and that if he was in a

good position to cover the ridge he'd probably get a shot.
That's just the way it worked out, too.
      Well, I'd better turn in. Exhausted and exhilarated.

Love, Fenton

Saturday

Dear Marge,
      Got my deer!
      To tell truth, I hadn't known what this sport all about
until now.
      My old buddies Pat and Retch showed me how to dress
out deer. Did it all by myself! Took me quite a while, but
Pat and Retch said to take my time and do it right and not
to worry about the camp chores because they were tired of
me hogging all the fun and from now on they get to share
them with me.

Best wishes, Fenton

Sunday

Marge,
      The three of us talked it over and decided we won't be
home for another week. Driving into town tomorrow for elk
tags. Will mail these letters to you then. Don't worry if you
don't hear from me for a while.

Cordially, Fenton Quagmire

Sweet Sweet
Sixteen

I had been sixteen years old for a long time now. Sixteen was an age I felt comfortable with. It was an age filled with exuberance, expectation, and surprise, with just a dash or two of madness. As is the nature of youth, I thought I would remain sixteen forever.

Vern and I had been fishing the river above the falls that day, and I remember snagging my favorite fly near the far bank and wading through the icy water up to my armpits to retrieve it. The force of the current lifted my feet and caused them to skitter dangerously over the rocks on the bottom, but I got the fly back and returned safely across the river, and Vern and I laughed because I hadn't been swept over the falls and drowned. Then we ate lunch, which was very soggy because I had been carrying it in the back of my fishing vest when I waded the river. We had to wring out the sandwiches before we could eat them. We cooked some of our smaller fish in a foil pan over a driftwood fire, seasoning them with salt, pepper, a whole cube of butter, and ashes and sand, and we ate the fish crisp and hot with our fingers. For dessert we ate handfuls of plump, sun-warmed huckleberries, the big fat reddish ones that grow on the tall bushes in the shade by the water. For dinner music, the river and the falls performed a symphony in the background, Mozart I think. Then it was time to climb the steep, winding trail up to the car on the logging road and head home.

"You know," I said to Vern, "I think I'll stay sixteen forever." He gave me a funny look and started up the trail.

When I got home that evening and squished into the kitchen, the family was gathered around the dining room table, one end of which was piled high with decoratively wrapped packages. "Surprise! Happy birthday! Happy birthday! Yea!"

"My birthday? Again, so soon? I thought we just celebrated it. Well, no matter, I do love my birthday. This looks a bit more festive than usual, though."

"Of course," my wife Bun said. "It's not every birthday you turn fifty."

"I suppose not," I said. "Hey, this is great. What a surprise! Let me at those presents. This one looks about the size of a fly reel. Now who could have guessed I needed a new . . . *what did you say?*"

"I said it's not every birthday you turn fifty."

"What is this, some kind of cruel joke? You know I'm not fif-fif . . . anywhere near that old. That's the age of old geezers, like grandfathers."

"Ha!" Bun said. "And just who do you think these four short people sitting here with the party hats on are?"

"*My* grandchildren? You're kidding! I thought they belonged to the neighbors."

"You have to start paying more attention," Bun said. "You're not sixteen anymore."

"I'm not? You mean this isn't a hoax? I really am fif-fif-fif . . ."

"That's right, fifty—the big five-0."

It was a shock. I suppose if I had aged gradually, it wouldn't have hit me so hard, old age. Say if, for example, the previous year I had been forty-nine and the year before that, forty-eight, and so on, I could have accepted such a dismal fate as inevitable. But it hadn't happened gradually. I jumped right from sixteen to fif-fif .·. . to *half a century old*. The jolt of it staggered me.

After the party, I went into the bathroom and looked in the mirror. Staring back at me was a person with gray hair, skin lined and blotched by the sun, a white mustache, a grizzled beard, and two chins, both of which began to quiver. So, it was true. This was not the face of a sixteen-year-old. This was a face that had been kicking around for half a century, the face of an old geezer—a grandfather!

Instantly my joints began to ache, my back to stiffen, my shoulders to slump. I felt my wrist—weak, fluttering pulse. I could practically hear the old ticker chugging and wheezing like a worn-out bilge pump. And to think, just a few hours before I had waded a cold river up to my armpits to retrieve an eighty-five-cent fly! Of course, I had still been only sixteen then. Something like that could kill an old geezer. I felt tired and weak and went into the den to take a nap, the first I'd taken since the age of three. From now on, I'd need lots of naps.

The next morning I got up feeling my age, which was old. I puttered about the house for a while.

"What in heaven's name are you doing?" Bun asked.

"Puttering about the house. Why?"

"Well, stop it! You don't know anything about puttering, and it's getting on my nerves."

"Got any stale bread around? Maybe I'll go sit on a park bench and feed the pigeons. It shouldn't be too hard to learn how to sit on a park bench and feed the pigeons. Where's the park, anyway?"

"We don't have a park. Go sit on the porch and feed the sparrows."

"I'd better put on a sweater. I wouldn't want to catch a chill."

While I was sitting on the porch, Raymond, a neighborhood kid, rode up on his bicycle. He is a shaggy, rumpled person, with more knees and elbows than average, or so it seems, possibly because his bike is much too small for him.

"Hey, whatcha doin' sittin' out here all by yourself on the porch? You look like some broken-down old geezer, ya know?"

"Beat it, Raymond. I don't need any cheering up."

"C'mon, I was just puttin' ya on. I heard ya turned fifty yesterday. So what! It ain't the end of the world."

"What do you know about it?"

"You can still have some fun. Like you could, uh, uh, no, I guess you couldn't do that, but you could, uh, uh, how about feed pigeons in the park? I admit it don't sound like a real blast to me, but lots of old guys seem to dig it."

"I've already thought about the pigeons, but there's no park around here. What do you want, Raymond? I know you didn't just come over here to shoot the breeze with a geeze."

"Well, now that you mention it, I thought you might advance me a couple bucks on mowin' your lawn."

"Raymond, you already owe me mowed lawns up into 1989. Say, what do *you* do when you're not speculating on lawn futures?"

"Ah, nothin' much. I hang around. What's to do?"

I couldn't believe he had said such a terrible thing. He's only sixteen. When I was sixteen, which happened to be the day before, I had 1,589,643 things to do, not even counting the things I didn't want to do. I was only up to 5,854 on the list, too, when I so suddenly got old.

"Raymond, don't talk like that. There are a million things to do. Actually, there are well over a million and a half things to do."

"All you old guys talk like that. Give me some examples."

"Well, you could take up fishing, for instance."

"That's one. What else?"

"What else! What do you mean, what else? Fishing is at least 800,000 things to do, all by itself. After you take up fishing, there's never again a moment when you don't have something to do. Take organizing a tackle box, for instance. You can spend your entire life just organizing a tackle box."

"You organize your tackle box a lot?"

"No, I've never organized it, but the point is it's always there waiting for me to organize it when I don't have something better to do. When you're a fisherman, though, there's always something better to do than organize a tackle box. Of course, you never have just one tackle box waiting to be organized. You have a tackle box for panfish, one for trout, one for bass, a couple for saltwater fishing, and so on. Over the years the contents of the various tackle boxes all get mixed up together. That's one of the things that make fishing such a wonderful challenge."

I then went on to tell Raymond about my long, unrequited love for fly-fishing and all the hundreds of different flies I still wanted to tie, as soon as I took lessons in the basics of fly-tying, and the fly rods I wanted to build as soon as I learned how, and all the famous and exotic lakes and streams I wanted to fish as soon as I accumulated the necessary cash. I told him about the purity of fly-fishing—the thrill of going up against wily trout with nothing more than a slender rod, some line, a tapered leader and a few flies, and that's all, except for the canoe, float tube, rubber raft, fly books, landing net, hip boots, boot waders, stocking waders, vest, extra rods, extra reels, thirty-seven different lines, salves, oils and ointments, hook sharpeners, wading staffs, and the ten dozen or so other essentials.

"Geez," Raymond said. "Do you have all the stuff you need for fly-fishing?"

"No, nobody has all the stuff you need for fly-fishing. It would require a warehouse to store just half of it. You see, no matter how much stuff you have for fishing, there's always more stuff you need. There's always new great stuff that you absolutely have to have, even though you didn't know you needed it before you saw it in a catalog. Fishermen spend hours poring over catalogs to find new stuff they can't possibly get along without. It's wonderful!"

"Yeah, fishing does sound like it might be fun."

"Fun? Raymond, I can't begin to tell you how fantastic it is—an evening hatch coming on, the light soft and mellow on the water, and you lay a dry fly soft as thistledown right next to the swirl of a big trout. Hey, let's go fishing right now! C'mon out to my warehouse and I'll get you outfitted."

"All right!"

"Listen, Raymond, you're going to love fishing. Never again in your whole life will you have nothing to do. I'll show you all the techniques, too—how to cast and tie knots and everything, even how to wring out sandwiches."

"Wait a minute," Raymond said. "I thought you had gotten too old for this sort of thing."

"Where did you get that idea? Sixteen isn't old, Raymond."

Down and Way Out
in Brazil

*He was an old man who fished alone in a skiff in the Gulf Stream
and he had gone eighty-four days now without taking a fish.*
—Ernest Hemingway, *The Old Man and the Sea*

Ever since the distant time of my youth and early manhood, Hemingway has been my hero, as a writer and as a hunter and fisherman. I particularly envied Hem's capacity for finding far-off and exotic places to fish, and I have tried to emulate him. For example, when Delroy Heap offered to let me fish the beaver ponds on his farm, I jumped at the chance. An opportunity like that may come only once in a lifetime, particularly when Delroy Heap happens to own the farm. If you knew Heap, you would understand, but you probably don't know him, which is no reason to think your life is a failure, believe me. Anyway, fishing Delroy Heap's beaver ponds was about as close as I've come to exotic fishing, let alone far-off, until one day last September.

The voice on the phone claiméd to be that of the editor of *Outdoor Life*, Clare Conley. "Pack your bags," the voice said. "I'm sending you to Brazil."

"Who is this really?" I said, chuckling. "Jim Zumbo? Ha, you can't fool me, Zumbo! I'd recognize your voice anywhere."

"This is not Zumbo, this is *Conley*! Now shut up and listen. I want you to accompany some pro football players and travel agents into the wilds of Brazil on a fishing trip."

Football players? Travel agents? Fishing in the wilds of Brazil? "You sure this isn't Zumbo?"

But it was actually Clare Conley and he was actually assigning me to do a story on fishing in Brazil. I dropped the phone and ran to tell my wife. "Bun! Bun!" I shouted. "I'm going to Brazil! Clare just assigned me to do a fishing story in Brazil!"

Bun gave me an astonished look. "Didn't I just wash and iron that shirt this morning? Now you've dribbled your pipe ashes all down the front!"

"Listen to what I'm saying! Clare just assigned me to do a fishing story in Brazil! I get to fish in a far-off, exotic place, just like Hemingway!"

"Quick!" she shouted. "Start growing your beard!"

"I'm trying," I said. "But I leave in three days. That's just enough time to learn to write like Hemingway!"

The six Americans hid out in a dark corner of the hotel bar, tossing back double shots of Alka-Seltzer. The Old Man ordered another round for everyone and after that there was only the sound of the Alka-Seltzer going *plop-plop*, *fizz-fizz* and occasionally a groan or a muffled burp. They were too tired to run anymore or even to shuffle along slowly. Their eyes were red and puffy with large dark bags under them and in some cases satchels and valises. The Americans had been in Rio de Janeiro, Brazil, for eighty-four days without taking any sleep and they now believed that the man known only as Carlos was trying to kill them.

"But why us?" Mac Beatty said. "All we want to do is catch a few fish." Mac was the owner and president of Travelwise, a travel agency in Portland, Oregon. He had fished all over the known world and a good deal of the unknown world but he had never come up against anything like Rio, where the only fish he had seen were on plates in restaurants, which is not the same as catching your own. "This is supposed to be a fishing trip, is it not?"

The Old Man laughed sardonically, which was not easy while gulping Alka-Seltzer. He explained the probable scenario that had set in motion the threat to their lives.

Carlos's boss in the Brazilian Tourism Authority, Embratur, had ordered the six Americans to be "taken care of" while they were in Rio.

Carlos nodded. "How do you want it done?"

"The usual Brazilian way," his boss said. "Party them to death."

The Americans knew if Carlos took them to one more party they were finished and all the Alka-Seltzer in the world would not save them. Their only hope was to get out of Rio fast and start the fishing before someone asked for whom the bell tolls and nobody could come up with a good answer except to look at the Americans and smile sadly.

The two quarterbacks looked as if they were done for anyway, and the Old Man wondered aloud if he shouldn't give them the last of his Rolaids and leave them behind while he and the travel agents escaped to the fishing camp.

"No way," said Cliff Stoudt, who was the great quarterback of the Birmingham Stallions. "You're not leaving Brian and me behind, although I wouldn't mind having the last of your Rolaids in any case."

"Yeah, we can make it," said Brian Sipe, who was the great quarterback of the New Jersey Generals. "You're not done for until you're done for."

After that the Old Man could see that Sipe was even worse than he had first thought and decided to finish off both quarterbacks quickly by doing his impersonation of Howard Cosell. They both cringed when he squeezed his nostrils together but said later they didn't realize he was getting ready to do his Cosell. His Cosell usually resulted in a clean kill but not always and sometimes he had to track the wounded into the bush and they would charge him, coming very fast and mean, and he would have to drop them with his Johnny Carson at close range.

But then Carlos came into the bar and saw the Americans slugging down double Alka-Seltzers. He complimented them for having eaten and drunk well and endlessly and for still showing some faint signs of life. "Tomorrow you can go fishing," he said. "Usually Americans do not survive nine Brazilian parties in a row, but you have. You have beaten me fairly and honorably and tomorrow you can go fishing."

"Good," the Old Man said. "I have been in Brazil eighty-four days now without catching either a wink or a fish."

"You have been in Brazil only three days," Carlos corrected him. "But tomorrow you will catch many fish in the Pantanal."

At the mention of Pantanal, the Old Man's spirits rose. He had read much literature about the Pantanal and knew that it was a paradise for zoologists and botanists and ecologists and, of course, fishermen. A great unspoiled wild place the size of Montana, the Pantanal teemed with strange and beautiful animals and with so many plants and flowers some of them had never even been named. Although the Old Man liked to think of it as a lovely, endless marsh, experts in such matters said the Pantanal was actually a lowland plain whose many broad, placid rivers gently flooded it during the rainy seasons. In other words, a marsh, thought the Old Man, who never really liked experts anyway.

"What time do we leave?" Ron Hart asked Carlos. Ron was an old South America hand, and president of Sportsman's Safaris out of Reno, Nevada. He and his partner Ted Kaphan were in Brazil setting up fishing and nature safaris on the Pantanal rivers for next summer, when they joined up with Mac, Cliff, Brian, and the Old Man.

"You leave for the fishing camp at dawn tomorrow," Carlos said. "Right after tonight's send-off party."

The Old Man was pronounced dead twice during the send-off party but revived both times asking, "Do we fish now?"

The next morning the Americans were flown a thousand miles inland to Cuiabá, the capital of the Brazilian state of Mato Grosso. From there, they were to be taken by bus into the Pantanal but were first rushed off to a welcoming party, where they were mistaken for zombies. After the party, they were allowed to sleep for three hours and then rousted out for a breakfast feast.

"Maybe they will let us rest for a day before going to the fishing camp," Brian said.

A tall young man appeared in the doorway. He wore the attire of a guide, including a large, wide-brimmed hat. The Americans stared sullenly at him.

"Excuse me," the guide said. "Let's go."

His name was Paulo and henceforth he would oversee the Americans' every waking moment during their expedition into the Pantanal. Eventually they would come to look upon him as a friend and one of the great guides of the world and a wonderful human being, but not until after making several unsuccessful attempts on his life.

On the long, dusty ride into the Pantanal, the Old Man was amazed at the lavish spectacle of nature stretching out as far as the sleep-sodden eye could see on both sides of the narrow, dike-like road. Ron Hart identified many of the birds for Brian and Cliff: garcas (herons), emas (small ostriches), siriema (large nonflying birds), jabiru (large storks), toucans, macaws, and so on. Where Ron left off, the Old Man took over.

"There's a duck," he said. "Some kind of weird duck." He hoped he wasn't being too technical.

Every few miles, Paulo would stop the bus. "Excuse me, let's go." Then the Americans would get off the bus and take pictures of alligators. They took 4,784 pictures of alligators.

Once, the Old Man made a serious mistake. He said to Paulo by way of idle conversation, "I wish I could get a good tight close-up of one of those 'gators."

"You want close-up of alligator?" Paulo cried. "Wait here!" Charging into the murky water, he began herding the alligators toward the Americans, and then there was much yelling and rushing about, although mostly by the Old Man, who was allergic to alligator breath.

A few miles down the road the bus stopped again. "Excuse me, let's go. Take pictures of dead alligator."

The alligator was very dead and had been that way a long time and was dried up and cracked and coming apart at the seams. Nobody wanted to take pictures of the dead alligator, since it already had enough problems.

"Yuck," Ted Kaphan said. "That's really awful."

"I've seen worse," Cliff Stoudt, the quarterback, said. "Tape him up and send him in for the second half."

The bus was hot and humid and the Old Man began to feel like the Gremlin that got cooked in the microwave. He stared out the window. Thousands of egrets blanketed the landscape like restless snow. Off in the distance, near the treeline, a small red deer with huge antlers browsed among wandering families of capybara, the world's largest rodent. The knobby eyes of alligators stared back at the Old Man from every pond of water. "The Pantanal is a very birdy and alligatory place," he thought. He wondered if it was also a very snakey place.

"Excuse me, let's go. Take pictures of anaconda."

The huge snake, disturbed from its nap in the middle of the road, did not want to have its picture taken. Before everyone had grabbed a camera and leaped off the bus, the anaconda had slithered off the road and down into a thick, boggy patch of brush. The Old Man thought his one chance to photograph an anaconda had vanished forever, but he did not yet know Paulo well.

The guide held up his hands to silence the cries of the disappointed. "Wait here. I be right back." Then he charged down into the brush after the anaconda.

Horrible sounds came from the brush: grunts, crashes, snarls, snaps, thumps, and thuds. The men on the road listened for sounds of severe squeezing. "Well," the Old Man thought, "no more 'Excuse me, let's go.'" And then Paulo lunged out of the brush, dragging the anaconda over his shoulder like a hawser. He threw the snake down in the middle of the astonished photographers, who leaped into the air and made ineffectual running motions. The snake, however, lay placidly on the road, too tired to squeeze anybody. It knew when it had met its match.

Late in the afternoon, the bus stopped abruptly at the Cuiabá River, which was a good thing because the road ended there and the river was full of piranha. At the fishing camp the men were given cabins with live frogs on the walls of the bathrooms. Later, Mac Beatty would step on a frog with his bare foot on the way to the bathroom in the dark and would wake the whole camp.

The men dropped their gear on the floor and fell into their beds and made deep rattling sounds with their throats. Finally, they would get some sleep.

"Excuse me, let's go." Paulo herded the Americans out to an all-night welcoming party thrown by the manager of the fishing camp, where they were once again mistaken for zombies. Brazilians love a good party.

The next morning the Americans finally got to go fishing. They got into two long, narrow, very tippy boats, and Indian guides took them far upriver very fast. The Old Man thought that maybe the reason the boats seemed so tippy was that the river was full of piranha. He remembered once seeing a film in which a cow waded into one side of a piranha river and came out the other side as a loose assortment of naked bones. The Old Man worried a great deal about the boat tipping over and wondered if he could swim to the near bank and survive to the extent that he could at least be identified by his dental X-rays.

The Cuiabá River was broad and languid and about the color of chocolate milk. The steep banks on both sides were backed by jungle. There were jaguars in the jungle but they were seldom seen because they come out only at night, and only a fool would want to be in the jungle at night. The Old Man was no fool.

Mac Beatty was in the bow of the Old Man's boat. It was good to have Mac in the bow of the boat, because otherwise the Old Man might have been there and the alligator might have got him. The Indian guide did not see the alligator on the bank and started to drive the boat in right beneath the ten-foot reptile. Mac did not see the alligator either, because he was busy fitting together his fly rod. Since the guide spoke only Portuguese, the Old Man yelled at him, *"Naranja sopa, por favor! Naranja sopa!"* Later he learned this meant, "Orange soup, please!" which may have explained why the guide looked puzzled and continued to drive the boat toward the alligator.

The alligator charged out over the top of Mac and bellyflopped into the water beside the boat. Mac instantly filled the air with karate chops but the alligator got away unharmed. Afterwards, Mac kept looking up to see what was about to jump on him, and that night he stepped on the frog with his bare foot.

Mac was a great fly fisherman and enjoyed the fight the big piranha put up against his light tackle. The guide thought Mac was crazy. He then demonstrated to Mac, Ted Kaphan, and the Old Man the proper way to catch fish. He baited a 10/0 hook with half a piranha and hurled the eighty-pound line and chunk of lead out into the river. Presently he jerked on the line and brought it in hand-over-hand very fast, clubbed the big fish, and dragged it into the boat. He had landed the fish in thirty seconds. He could not understand why the Americans liked to play with their fish.

The Americans caught many fish that morning, including piranha, dourado, pintado, piraracu, and others they could not identify. Ron Hart had told them the Pantanal rivers also held cachurro, peacock bass, filhote, and fish even Ron didn't know. The Old Man followed his practice of catching the fewest and smallest fish, so as not to embarrass his companions, but even his fish were big and strong and fought well, and after four hours the Old Man's arms ached from catching fish. Ron had said that the Cuiabá was by no means the best of the Pantanal's fishing rivers, and that there were many others much better, but the Old Man was satisfied with the Cuiabá and even elated. It beat the heck out of ol' Delroy Heap's beaver ponds.

At noon the guides took the Americans back to the fishing camp, where they ate piranha soup, which was very good and had just a tiny bite to it.

Then the Americans fell into their beds and slept for two hours straight, until Paulo awoke them and said it was time for the farewell party.

"What farewell?" Stoudt croaked. "We just got here!"

"Yeah," Kaphan said. "We're supposed to fish for three more days!"

"I'm just getting the hang of catching all these weird fish," Sipe said. "We can't leave now."

But Paulo said there had been a change of plans. The Americans had to be rushed back to Cuiabá for a round of parties. There appeared to be no end to Brazilian hospitality, and the Old Man thought he had never met a friendlier and warmer people. Still, he wanted to fish. By the time he returned home, he would have traveled a total of fourteen thousand miles to fish a total of four hours, which was not nearly enough. Hemingway would not have left after only four hours of fishing.

After the farewell party the next morning, the Old Man tried to detect sensation in his extremities but could find none. The other Americans, Sipe, Stoudt, Beatty, Hart, and Kaphan, stared forlornly at the river and remembered the great four hours of fishing they'd had there.

"Maybe there's been some mixup and they got it all straightened out and we'll get to fish for another three days," the Old Man said. "Look, here comes Paulo. He's smiling! I bet he's going to tell us we get to stay here and fish! What do you say, Paulo?"

"Excuse me, let's go."

Strange Encounters
of the Bird Kind

Many people go through life without having weird confrontations with birds, but I am not one of them. When I saw Alfred Hitchcock's suspense thriller *The Birds*, I thought it was a documentary. Several times during the movie, my wife screamed.

"Oh, that's so ghastly!" Bun said of one scene.

"Yeah, I know," I said. "It happened to me last week. See that big ugly bird pecking the guy's head? I think I recognize it."

Bun claims my attitude toward birds is neurotic. She likes birds. Once she hung up a hummingbird feeder outside our kitchen window and filled it with sugar water. For a week or so, even I enjoyed watching the birds slurp away at the feeder while I ate breakfast. It wasn't long, however, until word spread among the hummingbird population that there was a free handout to be had at the McManus house. Soon dozens of hummingbirds were flying holding patterns over our backyard, awaiting their turn at the sugar water.

I will admit that in the beginning the hummingbirds were orderly and well behaved, as anyone would be who had a sugar daddy like me on the string. After all, I was the one earning the bread to buy the sugar for their sugar water. It wasn't long until matters took a turn for the worse. One day the feeder ran dry and I forgot to pick up sugar at the store on my way home.

"Maybe you should go back to town and get the sugar," Bun said nervously. "The feeder has been empty all day."

I was indignant. "Listen, I'm not—I repeat, *not*—climbing into my car and driving six miles to buy sugar for a bunch of freeloading hummingbirds. They can wait until tomorrow."

"But," Bun said, glancing out the kitchen window, "they're becoming, well, sort of unruly."

Sure enough, they were. A dozen or more hummingbirds were hovering just outside the window, glaring in at us, their beady eyes aglitter with accusation.

"I don't like the looks of this," I said. "They're turning into a mob. There's no telling what they might do if they get out of hand. I've seen birds run amuck before. Maybe I will drive back to town for some sugar. Lock the doors and don't let anyone in, particularly if they're only an inch tall and wearing feathers."

It was a close call. Afterwards, I made sure we always had plenty of sugar on hand. When the hummingbirds went to the Caribbean for the winter, Bun and I heaved a sigh of relief and gave the feeder to the Johnsons, who live a couple of miles down the road. I never cared much for the Johnsons anyway.

The first birds I had trouble with were the family chickens when I was a young boy. They filled me with a sense of guilt that I never got over.

Every Saturday my grandmother and I would go out to the backyard, capture one of the chickens, and kill it for Sunday dinner. Gram, a stout, tough little old pioneer lady, did the actual killing. My job was to capture the luckless chicken.

"Git that one over there," she would order. As soon as the chicken saw her pointing at it, it would take off and try to make it to the county line. I would eventually run it down and start carrying it back to Gram, who waited at the chopping block, double-bitted ax in hand.

"Wait! Hold it!" the chicken would say to me. "You're making a terrible mistake! I didn't do anything! I'm innocent! Fred did it. You're mad about what happened last Tuesday, right? Well, that was Fred's fault. I saw him do it. I really did. Wait! Stop! Don't hand me over to that old lady! She's crazy!"

The part I played in these executions gave rise to such profound and enduring feelings of guilt that even as an adult I will often deliberately miss an easy shot at a game bird. Just as I am about to squeeze the trigger, a little voice inside me will plead, "Wait! Hold it!" and I will pull slightly off to the right or left of the target. My hunting companions, an uncouth and insensitive lot, respond to this explanation with raucous ridicule.

"Yeah, yeah," Retch Sweeney says. "And I suppose you helped your grandma chop the heads off clay pigeons, too!"

I haven't yet told him about the deeply disturbing childhood experience I had with a clay pigeon, because he probably would only scoff. There was also an extremely traumatic event involving the bull's-eye of a paper target, but I would rather not speak about it.

Birds have caused me the most problems, however. Take crows, for example. I crawl on my belly over ice and snow and sharp rocks to a place of concealment above a game trail. I crouch there, cramped and freezing, until months later I hear the sounds of deer or elk moseying up the trail. I ease off the rifle safety, curtail my breathing, gently bend my trigger finger to crack the ice from it. Any moment now. Suddenly there is a rush of wings. A crow flies into the tree above me.

"Holy smokes!" he squawks. "There's a guy down here with a gun! What are you doing with that gun? Hey, fellows, there's some joker crouched under this tree with a gun!" Instantly other crows take up the cry, reporting my presence to the world at large. The woods are in turmoil. I manage nevertheless to get off a single shot, but miss, which doesn't surprise me. When it's panicked and angling away from you at top speed, a crow is almost impossible to get in the cross-hairs.

A crow once caused my veracity to be called into question. My veracity at the time wasn't of particularly good repute anyway, and the crow didn't help matters. One day when I was about fifteen, I strolled aimlessly out of the house eating a cinnamon roll, and there right in front of me was a crow, perched on top of the family sedan. I was somewhat surprised, since the car was inedible and too big for the crow to steal. Continuing to amble toward the car, I expected the crow to fly off at any second. But it didn't. It just stood there, eyeing me and my cinnamon roll.

When I was right next to the car, the crow still hadn't flown. I became slightly nervous. The crow did a little shuffle with his feet, and then said in a clear voice, at least clear for a crow, "Hello." He sounded a bit like George Burns.

I was dumbfounded, never having met a bird that spoke human before.

"Hello," the crow said again, possibly thinking that I was slow-witted or hard of hearing.

I made a quick check to the left, right, and behind me, not wishing to be caught in the act of conversing with a bird, and then said, "Uh, hello."

The crow, it turned out, knew quite a few words, and we carried on something of a conversation, which, though it fell somewhat short of a discussion of politics or philosophy, was sufficient to cause me no little amazement. I must admit that at first I had difficulty identifying the particular topic of our little chat, but I soon deduced that for the crow's part it involved my cinnamon roll. This was communicated to me less from the words spoken than from the crow's cocking his head to eye the roll. I gave him half of it. He then flew off, and I never saw him again. At least I don't think I ever saw him again, since he bore an exact resemblance to all other crows. Occasionally I would yell "Hello!" to a passing crow, but he would look at me as if I must be mad, talking to a crow.

The crows, however, weren't the only ones to think I was, as my carpenter stepfather put it, "about a half-bubble off plumb." Immediately after the talking crow's departure, I rushed into the house to report the news. It was a Sunday, and the family was sitting around the dinner table playing cards.

"Guess what!" I shouted. "There was a crow standing on top of the car just now, and it knew how to talk!"

All eyes turned toward me, even as they narrowed to

slits of suspicion and disbelief. Lips tightened in preparation for directing slander at my person. But my mother, a woman who did not casually dismiss odd and rare phenomena as being beyond the realm of possibility, turned to my grandmother and said, "Whose bid?"

There was the time, too, when a vicious grouse charged out of the brush and broke my arm. I, of course, had seen ruffed grouse charge people before, but it was apparently a new experience for the horse I was riding, or so I judged from its attempt to climb a mature ponderosa pine. The horse was well up into the lower branches, when . . . But my psychiatrist says I'm to try not to think about it, and he's probably right.

The Outing

Afterwards, my mother, grandmother, and sister all wailed and gnashed their teeth and claimed that I had ruined them socially, a classic case of overreaction if I had ever seen one. You would have thought I was the first person in history to receive a dishonorable discharge from the Cub Scouts.

What initiated the whole disaster was Mr. Wilson's getting sick, or so he claimed, thus leaving our den of Cubs without an adult leader for our first overnight outing.

"I'll be the leader, then," I volunteered. "I know how to build fires and stuff."

"No, no," said Mrs. Slocum, the den mother. "That would never do. I'm afraid the trip must be postponed until some gentleman is available to lead you."

All the Cubs groaned, knowing it would take weeks or months for one of the mothers to browbeat her husband into leading us on an overnight outing.

"Hey!" I said. "I bet I know somebody who can take us!"

"You do?" said Mrs. Slocum. "That's wonderful! Why don't you ask the gentleman?"

Rancid Crabtree rocked his porch chair back against the slab wall of his shack, spanged a round of tobacco juice into a rusty coffee can, wiped his chin stubble on his sleeve, and said, "Tell me again, what was it Mrs. Slocum called me?"

"A gentleman."

Rancid nodded thoughtfully, apparently in agreement with this assessment of his character. "How come you and the widder Slocum was talkin' about me anyways?"

"Oh, why, she's the den mother of us Cubs. Her son Richie is a Cub and every week we meet at the Slocum mansion and tie knots and stuff. Boy, is she ever rich! They even got two cars."

"So?" Rancid said. "What about me? Where does me being a gentleman come in?"

"I was just getting to that. You see, we don't have an adult leader, a gentleman actually, to take us on an overnight camping trip. So I volunteered you."

Rancid's eyes narrowed to slits. "You gotcher nerve! If you thank Ah'm gonna nursemaid a bunch of you brats on a campin' trip, you got another thank comin'. Jist thankin' about it makes maw rheumatiz act up. Hand me thet quart jar of maw rheumatiz medicine."

I handed him the jar and watched him take a big enough swig to cure half the county of rheumatism.

"I thought you might feel that way about it," I said. "But you know how rich and pretty Mrs. Slocum is, and I thought maybe while you were in picking up us Cubs to go on the camping trip, you and Mrs. Slocum would get to talking and she would invite you in for coffee when we got back. You know, she doesn't have a man around the house to fix things for her, just ol' Richie, and he doesn't amount to much, so maybe she would say, 'Rancid, there's something wrong with the light in the bathroom. Do you suppose you could fix it for me?' And you would fix her light and she would be so grateful that after a while you and her would go out dancing together and after that maybe get married and you would be rich. But I suppose you're right. Well, so long, Rancid, I got to get home."

"*Wait!*"

I hardly recognized Rancid when his old truck rattled up in front of the Slocum mansion the following Saturday. He was wearing new bib overalls, an old suit jacket, a reasonably white shirt, and his battered felt hat. His face was clean-shaven and pink from scrubbing.

"Rancid!" I shouted. "You look great!"

"Don't holler," he said, wincing. "It harts maw hide."

Mrs. Slocum swept down the walk from the mansion holding out her hand. "I'm so pleased to meet you, Mr. Crabtree. Pat has told me so much about what a fine woodsman you are. I just know you will teach the boys some wonderful nature lore. It's divine of you to take the boys camping."

Rancid blushed, shaking her hand. "Waal, Ah was a Grub once mawsef!"

"Cub," I corrected him.

"Cub, Ah mean."

"Oh, you're so amusing, Mr. Crabtree. May I call you Rancid?"

"Shore."

By then all the other Cubs had loaded the gear into the

back of the truck and were yelling for us to get started. Rancid and I got in the cab and the other boys climbed on behind. Mrs. Slocum took out a dainty handkerchief and waved it at us as we roared off down the street.

"Have a good time, all," she called after us.

Rancid grinned all the way out of town. "You see how she wanted to call me Rancid right off," he said. "Ah guess Ah ain't lost it yet!"

"Lost what?" I said.

"Ain't none of yer bidness."

Rancid drove up along Pack River until we came to a Forest Service campground. He pulled in and stopped.

"Okay, Grubs, this is it. Git off and set up camp."

The Cubs stared at the campground.

"We don't want to camp here, Mr. Crabtree," Robert said. "This is practically civilization. We want to climb to the top of that mountain, where it's wild."

"Yeah," Henry joined in. "We want to climb the mountain. If we camp here, we won't even get to carry our packs. It won't be like a real camping trip."

The rest of us Cubs shouted agreement.

Rancid slapped his leg. "Gol-dang, what am Ah thankin' of? 'Course it wouldn't be like real campin'. It's been at least a week since the b'ars et thet pore fella up on the mountain, but they's probably not real hungry already. Gitcher packs on and let's go."

"Wait a minute," said Richie. "This campground seems pretty good to me. Why don't we stay right here, close to the truck?"

The other guys said the campground was looking better to them all the time. "Who wants to climb an old mountain anyway?" said Norm.

"I didn't hear anything about bears eating anybody," I said to Rancid.

"Shut yer yap and go fix a fahr," he said. "Ah got to step behind them trees over thar and prepare maw rheumatiz fer a night on the hard, cold ground."

As soon as camp was set up, the Cubs started begging Rancid to teach them some nature lore.

"What kind of insects are these, Mr. Crabtree?" Delbert asked.

"Jist yer basic wild bugs," Rancid said, cutting a chaw of tobacco from his plug.

"What's the name of that bird flying around up there?" Melvin asked.

Rancid squinted up at the sky. "Iggle—a baldheaded iggle. Bet you Grubs never seed a baldheaded iggle before. Went bald from baby iggles askin' it so many questions. Now why don't you boys go poke sticks in the fahr or some-thin'?"

That night as we sat around incinerating marshmallows, Rancid hunched over the campfire with a blanket around his shoulders. "This was yer idear," he growled to me out of the corner of his mouth. "The gol-dang skeeters is eatin' me alive. Ah know'd Ah shouldn't of took no bath! Even iffen Ah wake up daid in the mornin', Ah'm gonna hunt you down and whup the tar outta ya fer gittin' me inter this mess."

"But . . ." I started to say.

"Mr. Crabtree," Delbert broke in, "why don't you tell us some ghost stories? Something real scary!"

"Don't know no ghost stories," Rancid muttered.

"Don't you know any scary stories at all?" somebody asked.

Rancid thought for a moment. "*Hmmmm.*" It was his

wicked *hmmmm.* "Waal, Ah know one *true* story thet's purty skeery. But it'd bore you Grubs. Naw, Ah don't want to tell it."

"Tell it, Mr. Crabtree, tell it!"

"Oh, all right. It seems thar was this woodcutter lived up in these hyar mountains. Might still be runnin' 'round these parts, fer all Ah know. Anyhow, he went crazy. Fust thang anybody know'd he'd gone crazy, these campers was found all cut up in itty-bitty pieces. Crazy ol' woodcutter must have snuck up on 'em in the dark of night . . . What was thet? You Grubs hear somethin'? Oh, probably warn't nothin'. Now this crazy ol' woodcutter . . ."

Driving back toward town an hour later, Rancid hummed and sang and beat time to his own tune on the steering wheel, every so often interrupting the tune to go "heh heh."

"There wasn't any crazy old woodcutter, was there?" I said.

"Who knows? Might hev been. Dum dee dum dum *heh heh.* Now here's maw plan. We go back to maw place, you and t'other Grubs camps out by maw shack, and in the mornin' Ah hauls ya all back to town and nobody knows the difference."

I tried to ignore the premonition unfolding in my innards.

Presently we came to a roadhouse ablaze with lights. "Whoa, hoss!" Rancid said, hitting the brakes. "The night's still young. Let's see what's happenin' in thar. Ah'll stand you and t'other Grubs to some pops."

Looking back, I suppose our little group marching into the roadhouse must have presented something of a spectacle, the tall, lanky mountain man trailed by what appeared to be eight pint-sized Union cavalrymen.

"You can't bring those kids in here," the barman barked at Rancid.

"Ah thought Ah jist did," Rancid replied calmly. "Set 'em up a round of pops."

Snarling, the bartender set a row of glasses along the bar and, without asking our preference, filled them with orange pop. Rancid wandered over to a card game being played by some hard-looking men. "What do ya call this game?" he asked.

"Stud poker," the dealer said.

"Take long to larn it?" Rancid asked. "Mebbe Ah'll set in fer a hand."

"Rancid," I said, "we'd better go. We're supposed to be camping."

"Don't pester me, boy. Ah'm jist gonna play a few hands to see if Ah can git the hang of this, whatcha call it, stub poker? You Grubs go shoot some pool or play the slot machines, but stay outta trouble."

All the Cubs agreed later that it was one of the more interesting evenings of our lives. Delbert said it was just like in the movies, and Melvin said no, it was even better. They were referring to the fracas that started when one of the cardplayers yelled something about cheating, and the card table got knocked over, and Rancid shouted, "Quick, fetch me one of them pool cues!" And we all thought he wanted the cue to play pool with!

One by one the parents of the Cubs came down to the sheriff's office in the predawn hours to pick up their sons. It was a memorable scene. I particularly remember Mrs. Slocum coming in, snatching Richie by the hand, and heading for the door without saying a word to me or Rancid, who was arguing with one of the deputies. I knew right then that my career in the Cub Scouts was over. Then Rancid noticed Mrs. Slocum dragging Richie out the door.

"Ma'am!"

Mrs. Slocum stopped, turned slowly, as if she had been quick-frozen and was coming unthawed. "Yessss, Mr. Crabtree?" she said through her teeth.

"Uh, ma'am," said Rancid, "Ah suppose this means you won't be wantin' me to fix yer bathroom light."

I, the Hunted

Five minutes more and I would once again have escaped to relative safety. From the baying sounds, I knew the pack had picked up my trail and was now circling to my rear. The scrawny tree into which I attempted to blend like the bark itself offered no cover from that direction. Ahead of me lay an open grassy area. I had no choice but to cross it and seek concealment among some bushes on the far side. Employing the technique of the scurrying squat, I raced into the open—and right into the trap that had been laid for me on the grounds of Delmore Blight Grade School. Curses!

Rupert Skraggs, seemingly appearing out of nowhere, snapped his famous half-nelson on me. Through bulging eyeballs I saw the clever ruse with which he had tricked me— a blind assembled out of a group of quivering fourth-graders! His baying pack, consisting of Wilfred Hogmire, Fats Moon, and Clarence Simp, had been but a diversionary tactic to flush me into the open.

"You boys stop your fighting this instant or I'll send you to the principal," screamed the harried teacher condemned to playground supervision.

Even as Skraggs sighed and loosened his half-nelson, dropping me with a plop to the ground, I wondered at the rarity of playground supervisors who could distinguish between a fight and a beating-up.

"You lucked out this time, punk," Skraggs snarled. "But I'll get you after school."

"Oh, yeah?" I croaked, massaging my Adam's apple back into something resembling its original shape. "You don't scare me, Skraggs." I chose not to explain why I had spent the lunch hour imitating the bark of a tree.

"We'll see about that, you puny little rat!" Skraggs snarled.

"Yeah, and you got dandruff," I retorted. I made a mental note to work on my repertoire of insults. *Dandruff*, for pity's sake!

The bell rang, mercifully ending the lunch hour.

In retrospect, I now see that Rupert Skraggs taught me some important lessons. During my grade-school years, when I was still too young to hunt, he provided me with the opportunity to serve an apprenticeship as the hunted. Nothing so well instructs a hunter about hunting as once having been hunted himself. Off and on during the years I was incarcerated in grade school, Rupert Skraggs would hunt me for weeks at a time. I learned to move quickly, silently, covering my trail as I went. I learned to take on the protective coloration of my surroundings, whether the school playground, a vacant lot, or the movie theater. I even learned to catch Skraggs's scent when he moved upwind of me, although anyone who sat near him in a hot, humid classroom would scarcely be impressed by this achievement.

Skraggs had lain in ambush for me in fourth grade.

When I was in second, he was in fourth, when I was in third, he was in fourth, and when I finally made it to fourth, Skraggs was still there, as if waiting on stand for me to come to him. He was then promoted right along with the rest of us, just as if he knew how to read and write. I suppose the reason for his promotion related directly to the teacher's dislike of having a fourth-grader who sported a mustache and sideburns.

I should mention here that although Skraggs routinely beat up the rest of us boys, apparently looking upon it as an inexpensive hobby, he did so usually without malice, almost cordially. What his beating-ups lacked in pain, they made up for in humiliation. You might smile and wink debonairly at a pretty girl flouncing by after school, but the effect was lost if your head at that moment was protruding from one of Skraggs's half-nelsons.

Some of my friends held the opinion that it was best and safest to go along good-humoredly with Skraggs's beating-ups. The idea was to act as if it were all in good fun and a welcome relief from your otherwise boring existence. I never liked that idea. Perhaps that is why Skraggs took such a serious dislike to me. He considered me a spoilsport.

I once made the mistake of trying to reason with Skraggs.

"Listen, Rupert, you're not proving anything by beating me up all the time. Why do it?"

He thought a moment, then suddenly brightened, as if having hit upon a profound truth. " 'Cause it's fun, dummy!" *POW!*

In my appeal to reason, I had failed to take into account the entertainment factor.

I then decided to challenge Skraggs to a fair fight—my friends Bruce, Peter, and I against Skraggs. We confronted him on his way home from school one day.

"Hold it right there, Skraggs," I said. "I got a bone to pick with you."

Skraggs turned, rolling up his sleeves over his burley arms.

"Yeah? You and who else?"

"I'll tell you who—me and Bruce and . . ."

I was distracted by the sound of running footsteps diminishing into the distance.

"Uh, well, me and my friend . . ."

The sound of another set of running footsteps diminished into the distance.

"So, Rupert. How ya doin' today?"

Six blocks away I managed to shake Skraggs off my tail, but I knew the next time he caught me the beating-up would be a good deal less cordial.

Most of my classmates harbored the hope that one day Skraggs would make the mistake of beating up one of us badly enough that he would be sent to reform school. I was the odds-on favorite to gain status as his ultimate victim. I could tell from the looks my classmates gave me, looks of sympathy, looks of relief.

It finally became clear to me what I would have to do. I would have to murder Skraggs. Every day during the geography lesson, I would plot the perfect murder. It would be simple but ingenious. The police would be baffled:

INSPECTOR: First time I've run into a case like this. The culprit is obviously a brilliant but diabolical chap. Note, Watson, the clever use of a homemade arrow, impossible to trace.

WATSON: The arrow killed him, then?

INSPECTOR: Not really. The tip of the arrow was dipped in a highly poisonous substance. My guess is it's spoiled potato salad—deadly stuff. My own mother warned me about it.

WATSON: But what's this contraption?

INSPECTOR: A framework of old two-by-fours and fence-posts cleverly constructed at the proper height to hold the crossbow. Note how the structure is covered with weeds to conceal it. The string, you see, leads from the trigger on the crossbow to the victim's bicycle seat. Any pressure on the bicycle seat releases the arrow. Absolutely ingenious! Do we know, Watson, if the victim had any enemies?

WATSON: Yes, sir. Several dozen of them are at this moment out in the street, cheering.

I never did get around to murdering Skraggs, although there was some mystery about the framework of two-by-fours and fenceposts discovered in the brush near his house. It was probably just as well. As the years passed, a peculiar thing happened. Skraggs began to shrink! By seventh grade, I was the same size as my old adversary. By the time we reached high school, I towered over him. Oddly, the more he shrank, the nicer and more ingratiating he became.

I am pleased to say that I am not the sort of person to hold a grudge. Even though I could have taken my revenge by beating up Skraggs anytime I felt the urge, I did not do so. In fact, I often took him pheasant hunting with me, just to show him my appreciation for all he had taught me in my years as his quarry.

My one disappointment with him as a hunting companion was that although he learned to retrieve nicely, he never caught on to pointing worth a darn. On the other hand, I sort of enjoyed his whining when the late duck season opened.